D0410473

Everything To Play For

99 POEMS ABOUT SPORT

WITHDRAWN FROM STOCK

WITHDRAWN FROM STOCK

Everything To Play For

99 POEMS ABOUT SPORT

Edited by
John McAuliffe

Foreword by
Sonia O'Sullivan

Poetry Ireland Éigse Éireann

Leabharlann
6543434
Contae Na Midhe

Poetry Ireland Ltd / Éigse Éireann Teo gratefully acknowledges
the assistance of The Arts Council / An Chomhairle Ealaíon
and The Arts Council of Northern Ireland, along with our partners
The Croke Park, Dublin.

LOTTERY FUNDED

THE CROKE PARK

DOYLE COLLECTION · DUBLIN

**DUBLIN'S ICONIC
SPORTING HOTEL**

The moral right of the copyright holders has been asserted.

ISBN: 978-1-902121-57-4

DESIGN: Niall McCormack *www.hitone.ie*

First published by Poetry Ireland, 2015

www.poetryireland.ie

Contents

FOREWORD   xi

INTRODUCTION   xv

1   TENNIS & TABLE TENNIS

Paul Durcan	*A Spin in the Rain with Seamus Heaney*	2
Vona Groarke	*The Game of Tennis in Irish History*	6
Iggy McGovern	*The Difference*	8
Fergus Allen	*Tennis in Wicklow*	9
Paul Muldoon	*How to Play Championship Tennis*	10

2   GAELIC FOOTBALL

Pádraig J. Daly	*Footballer*	14
Seamus Heaney	*Station Island, VII*	15
Gabriel Fitzmaurice	*Munster Football Final 1924*	20
Bernard O'Donoghue	*Munster Final*	21
Noel Monahan	*The Football Field*	22
Seamus Heaney	*The Point*	23
Patrick Deeley	*Minding Goal*	24
Michael Hartnett	*Reconstructionists*	26
Brendan Kennelly	*The Madness of Football*	28
Brendan Kennelly	*A Religious Occasion*	29
Peter Fallon	*Hay*	30
Bernard O'Donoghue	*Croke Park or Ballylee, 1989*	32
Martina Evans	*A Man's World*	35
Paul Durcan	*Sport*	36

CONTENTS

3 HORSE RACING

Peggie Gallagher	*The Three Card Trick Man*	42
Tom French	*The Race Field*	43
Gerard Fanning	*Laytown Races, 1959*	44
Padraic Fallon	*Gowran Park, Autumn Meeting*	45
W.B. Yeats	*At Galway Races*	46
Tom Duddy	*The Racing Festival*	47
Frank Ormsby	*Action Replays*	48
Mary Noonan	*Lone Patrol*	50
F.R. Higgins	*The Old Jockey*	52
Martina Evans	*The Wide World*	53

4 GOLF, PITCH & PUTT

Matthew Sweeney	*The Yellow Golf Ball on the Lawn*	58
Maurice Riordan	*He Begins With A Line by Sandy Lyle*	60
Conor O'Callaghan	*Pitch & Putt*	61
David Wheatley	*Moonshine*	62
John O'Donnell	*Poetry*	63
Dermot Bolger	*Remembering Certain Golf Holes*	64

5 HANDBALL & BOWLS

Seamus Heaney	*Squarings, XI*	68
Martin Dyar	*Handball Legend*	69
Greg Delanty	*After Viewing The Bowling Match at Castlemary, Cloyne, 1847*	70

6 SOCCER

Brendan Kennelly	*Manager, Perhaps*	74
Robert Greacen	*Goals*	75

David Park	George Best	76
Miriam Gamble	Tinkerness	77
Elaine Feeney	Ryan Giggs is a Ride	79
Paul Durcan	The Beautiful Game	81
Alan Gillis	If There was Time All Day to Wait	83
Rita Ann Higgins	Ireland Is Changing Mother	86
Paul Muldoon	Soccer Moms	88
Tom French	The Fathers Raising the Nets for the Last Game of the Season: a Triptych	90

7 RUNNING

John O'Donnell	Sports Day	94
Theo Dorgan	Running with the Immortals	96
Colette Bryce	Great North	98
Gerry Murphy	Keeping in Shape	100

8 CYCLING

Vincent Woods	Bicycle	104
Louis MacNeice	The Cyclist	106
John F. Deane	Bikes	108

9 FISHING, ARCHERY, FALCONRY & SKIING

Sebastian Barry	Two Brothers Up	112
Patrick Deeley	Fisherman	113
Ciaran Carson	Finding the Ox	115
Caitríona O'Reilly	The Curée	116
Paula Cunningham	Seeing Things	118

CONTENTS

10 INDOOR / OUTDOOR SPORTS & GAMES

Conor O'Callaghan	Green Baize Couplets	122
Paul Durcan	The 2003 World Snooker Championship	124
Louis MacNeice	Soap Suds	127
Louis MacNeice	Darts & Shove halfpenny	128
Seamus Heaney	Squarings, III	129
Gerard Smyth	Marbles	130
Matthew Sweeney	The Glass Chess Set	131

11 BOXING

Daragh Breen	Boxer	134
Patrick Kavanagh	A Knight at the Tournament	135
Michael Longley	The Boxers	136
Declan Ryan	Rope-a-Dope	137

12 WATER SPORTS

Eiléan Ní Chuilleanáin	The Last Glimpse of Erin	142
Sinéad Morrissey	Forty Lengths	143
Pat Boran	Learning to Dive	144
Leontia Flynn	Saturday in the Pool	146
Conor O'Callaghan	The End of the Line	148
Gerry Murphy	Swimming Out	149
Mary O'Malley	Surfing	151

13 HURLING & CAMOGIE

Paul Durcan	The One-Armed Crucifixion	154
Michael Gorman	Camogie	155

Patrick Kavanagh	*Camogie Match*	156
John FitzGerald	*Ecstasis*	157
Liam Murphy	*Donal Foley Played Hurling with My Father*	158
Bryan MacMahon	*A Song for Christy Ring*	160
Theo Dorgan	*Learning My Father's Memories*	162
Billy Ramsell	*Lament for Christy Ring*	164
Enda Wyley	*On My Father's Birthday*	168
Tom French	*A Laminated Hurley*	171

14 AMERICAN SPORTS

Frank McGuinness	*American Football in Booterstown Park*	174
Conor O'Callaghan	*Game Night*	176
Greg Delanty	*Tagging the Stealer*	177
Paul Muldoon	*Chunkey*	179

15 RUGBY & CRICKET

Louis MacNeice	*Rugby Football Excursion*	182
John O'Donnell	*Team Photo*	185
Thomas McCarthy	*The Cappoquin Cricket XI*	186
Gerard Fanning	*Offering the Light*	188

16 THE DOGS

Paul Muldoon	*At Master McGrath's Grave*	192
Ciaran Carson	*Night Music*	194
Maurice Riordan	*The Holy Land*	195

ACKNOWLEDGEMENTS

198

Foreword

YOU MIGHT wonder why I'm writing the foreword to a poetry anthology, even if it is poetry inspired by sport. When I was told about this book my first thoughts went to all those times when people commented that watching me run was like poetry in motion, like a gazelle in the distance eating up the ground.

And that is exactly how it is for me, particularly if I'm out for a run on my own. People often ask me what do you think about when you're out running. It's one of the hardest questions to answer, as so many thoughts go through my mind, so many great ideas if only I could break them down into a little rhyme that I could recall and share when standing in front of an audience. My thoughts drift as I reflect on recent events or recall a medal-winning run or great training session. Days when everything just flowed with effortless strides. When I returned home, if only I could have ordered my thoughts and put them on paper! But they were soon dispersed as I was brought back to the reality of daily life once the early morning run was over.

Sport is such that those immersed in it will never be satisfied, rarely will you get the perfect day and even when you do it drives you on to achieve more. As athletes we all work hard training and preparing for the events that lie ahead, we all have the ingredients to get a great result, but it's how you mix those ingredients together and the care and patience you take in training that will deliver the perfect result.

Poetry too I'm sure needs such patience and care. It's a form of the written word that can be interpreted in many ways, just like a boxing match or an Olympic race: if you have a room full of people watching, they will all predict the outcome in their own way, and believe that if different decisions were made then the outcome would have been different. When the race is over we can all look back and think, what could I have done differently? Even if you win you still think you could've run faster, or played better, or tried a little harder.

I have competed at the highest levels in sport and now I take part in a really wide range of activities. Only recently over the course of a weekend I climbed the highest mountain in Ireland and cycled the Beara Peninsula. The sheer beauty carried me up and down the hills alongside people of all abilities taking part and immersing themselves in sport.

The Olympic motto 'Faster, Higher, Stronger' was proposed in 1894 by Pierre de Coubertin, founder of the modern Olympic Games. He said, 'These three words represent a programme of moral beauty. The aesthetics of sport are intangible.' That aesthetic is easier to feel than it is to explain, and Coubertin also went on to add to this motto, in 1908, 'The most important thing is not to win but to take part.'

I understand more now about the enjoyment and satisfaction of taking part, of being involved, sharing and inspiring the next generation. We can't all be Olympic champions but we can all get out there, take part and feel the joy and satisfaction so often seen when watching great sporting feats and achievements, many of which have inspired the poems that are compiled for your enjoyment in this wonderful book.

Sonia O'Sullivan

Bright Particular Star

'I USED to run with my friend when he was training to keep him in company. He would give me a long start and soon overtake me.' So wrote W.B. Yeats of his teenage athletics training, and then, in relation to his enthusiasm for sport: 'I followed the career of a certain professional runner for months, buying papers that would tell me if he had won or lost. I had seen him described as "the bright particular star of American athletics," and the wonderful phrase had thrown enchantment over him.'

Almost everyone has similar stories about 'bright particular stars' they followed, or still follow, runners or hurlers, a jockey or footballer or tennis player whose excellence shines out week after week and from year to year. And who is to say that Yeats's devotion to the solitary art of writing was not in some way formed by his youthful interest in athletics? The discipline, practice and exposingly public occasions of the writing life do have *something* in common with the athlete's, and may explain why so many Irish poets have been drawn to sport. Given the hundreds of poems on the subject, it is striking that no anthology like this has been published before now.

Sport has long been at the heart of people's relationships in Irish life: it is one of the ways in which we stay in touch and one of the pleasures of our continuing conversations with one another. And sport's the stuff of family lore – the wrong turn at Ballybrit that led to Connemara instead of the Galway Races, the ex who came good with tickets, the All-Ireland winner throwing an American football on the beach one summer's day. And it continues to be the better, *social* part of many working lives, whether at a workplace gym, a group that meets for Sunday runs, or increasingly slow-paced Monday evening five-a-sides on deteriorating pitches, where knee injuries, parenthood and job changes increasingly encroach. Some poets have wondered, then, at how sports get compartmentalized and separated from high art: Bernard O'Donoghue asks, one September day, 'Should we go up to the All-Ireland final / or repeat another tried pilgrimage / [...] to Yeats's Tower?', but this is a choice which many of the poems here refuse to make. Instead, these poets, like O'Donoghue, bring together the private moment of the lyric poem with the more public occasion of the sporting event.

Many of the poems collected in this anthology respond to the way that sport has formed a kind of alternative national narrative: maybe it is true that we measure out our lives in relation to sporting events, from 1978 and the sheer, quick-witted imagination of Mikey Sheehy's lobbing a free over Paddy Cullen; to 1979, the year Brady set up the Cup winner against Utd; to 1982 with Seamus Darby and his two wild leaps after his late goal; the midnight session of tea and biscuits as Dennis Taylor peered through his big glasses at each eminently missable black in 1985, the same year Barry McGuigan defeated Eusebio Pedroza; Stephen Roche turning a corner seconds behind Pedro Delgado in 1987, crossing the line and collapsing and needing oxygen (and his great peer Sean Kelly dominating the classics all that decade); David O'Leary's penalty in 1990; Sonia running away from Ribeiro in 1995 in Gothenberg (and her great race with Gabriela Szabo in Sydney in 2000); 1999 is Ben O'Connor pointing from the sideline in the rain, and so on…

Poets have been drawn to those moments when a sport-star or event brings us out of ourselves and into an imagined community: in this book there are exalting tributes to George Best (and Ryan Giggs), Sonia O'Sullivan and Paula Radcliffe, Ken Doherty and Master McGrath. And Christy Ring who, in Billy Ramsell's poem, becomes a CGI marvel: 'his stick of ashy liquidity / that's rippling, eel-flexible, alive. / / And now his body it is liquid too, / an impressionist version of itself / as he slights the wall of three defenders, / pours himself through some improbable gap / and on the other side re-solidifies.'

These poems take a vicarious pleasure in the feats of sportsmen and sportswomen: the thrill and intensity of bringing work to a very high level, the sense of achievement in preparing for and completing an event. They somehow find and communicate exactly how we feel about the pleasure of working at full capacity. But sport is more than a heroic enterprise and the 'actual' national narrative also figures strongly in these poems: sport is intricately interwoven into every aspect of Irish society. The backdrop to the Parnells playing tennis in 1871 is, for Vona Groarke, 'incident and outrage', while Gabriel Fitzmaurice observes the 'open wounds' of the Civil War recede as team-mates line out together so that 'on Con Brosnan's safe conduct Sheehy takes the field.' Seamus Heaney's great long poem *Station Island* powerfully centres on a figure whose humanity is brought home in lines like: 'he was still that same / rangy midfielder in a blue jersey / and starched pants, the one stylist on the team, // the perfect clean, unthinkable victim', and Rita Ann Higgins imagines a changing Ireland where 'the Namibian gods and the Bally Bane Taliban / are bringing the local yokels / to their menacing senses / and scoring more goals than Cú Chulainn.'

But if sport lends itself to the marking of public occasions, *more often* the poets find angles that would not make the news. There is a reason why in their poems about horse-racing, both Peggie Gallagher and Tom Duddy begin with the line, 'The reason I come here is not the horses': what they are after instead is caught by Padraic Fallon's beautiful images of a winter meeting in Gowran Park, 'A low sun noses through the damps; / The trees are bare down to the stumps; / A mist can spring up white as lime.' And Gerard Fanning's take on the Laytown Races is similarly original and atmospheric as it catches the sporting event's potential:

'I'll soon be called to eat or swim. / The horses are held back with bunting. / A langourous tide is coming in.'

Going to an event, reporting what someone said – about who played well or who performed badly, or even participating yourself, these poems are themselves 'bright particular stars' which definitively record the ways in which sport helps us to know one another. In particular, this book is full of affecting and affectionate poems about children and parents attending events together, where sport acts as a kind of knot binding one generation to another. It is not always positive: witness Paul Durcan's unforgettable image of days spent fielding *sliotars* driven at him by his father as a 'one-armed crucifixion', but see also Enda Wyley's poem for her father remembering days spent 'chasing after the *sliotar* / your hurley gives to those holiday waves', and Michael Longley's elegy for his brother which begins 'We were combatants from the start. Our dad / bought us boxing gloves when we were ten' and ends, 'I'll tie your gloves. Shall we fight again?' And Tom French's description of an under-age match describes the kind of good productive space that sport, like a poem, makes for people to live in, a dreamed-up house we must mind and defend and re-make again and again:

They will come again, when they've put this summer
behind them, and feel grateful again for these nets,
without which they would be men in the midst of grass

bellowing *"House! House! House!"* where no house is,
at sons running to forestall what is bound to happen next.

If French's poem shows us that sport involves parents and children and a community of activists and umpires and pitch-minders and scouts and cheer-leaders and armchair generals and advocates and supporters, then editing this anthology has reminded me that poetry is not just writers and readers: it too is a team sport. I would like to acknowledge Paul Rouse for the initial idea for this book, and the assistance of Poetry Ireland's analysts, scouts and organisational impresarios, Muireann Sheahan, Paul Lenehan, Elizabeth Mohen, Maureen Kennelly and in particular Krystal LaDuc and Catherine Ward, whose encouraging ability to come up with ideas, and track down and discover poems, made this anthology into the book you have in your hands.

John McAuliffe

Tennis & Table Tennis

PAUL DURCAN

A Spin in the Rain
with Seamus Heaney

You had to drive across to Donegal town
To drop off a friend at the Dublin bus
So I said I'd come along for the spin –

A spin in the rain.
Bales of rain
But you did not alter your method of driving,

Which is to sit right down under the steering wheel
And to maintain an upwards-peering posture
Treating the road as part of the sky,

A method which motoring correspondents call
Horizontal-to-the-vertical.
The hills of Donegal put down their heads

As you circled upwards past their solitary farmhouses,
All those agèd couples drenched over firesides,
Who once were courting couples in parked cars.

You parked the car in Donegal town and we walked the
        shops –
Magee's and The Four Masters Bookshop.
You bought ice-cream cones. I bought women's magazines.

We drove on up through the hills past Mountcharles
And Bruckless and Ardara.
There was a traffic jam in Ardara,

Out of which you extricated yourself
With a jack-knife U-turn on a hairpin bend
With all the bashful panache of a cattle farmer –

A cattle farmer who is not an egotist
But who is a snail of magnanimity,
A verbal source of calm.

Back in the Glenties you parked outside the National School
Through whose silent classrooms we strayed,
Silent with population maps of the world.

Standing with our backs to a deserted table-tennis table
We picked up a pair of table-tennis bats
And, without being particularly conscious of what we
        were at,

We began to bat the ball one to the other
Until a knock-up was in progress,
Holding our bats in pen grips.

So here we are playing a game of ping-pong
Which is a backdrop to our conversation
While our conversation is a backdrop to our game.

We are talking about our children and you speak
Of the consolation of children when they grow up
To become our most trusted of all companions.

I could listen to you speak along these lines
For the rest of the day and I dare say
You could listen to me also speak along my lines:

I have always thought that ping-pong balls –
Static spheres fleet as thoughts –
Have flight textures similar to souls'.

I note that we are both of us
No mean strikers of the ball and that, although
We have different ways of addressing the table –

Myself standing back and leaping about,
Yourself standing close and scarcely moving –
What chiefly preoccupies us both is spin.

As darkness drops, the rain clears.
I take my leave of you to prepare my soul
For tonight's public recital. Wishing each other well.

Poetry! To be able to look a bullet in the eye,
With a whiff of the bat to return it spinning to drop
Down scarcely over the lapped net; to stand still; to stop.

VONA GROARKE

The Game of Tennis in Irish History

Blame Lady Alice Howard and her diary of 1873
patrolling the white line around the one green space
at Shelton Abbey where the Parnells, Charlie and Fanny,

banter in and back, skirting the net, filling the hours
between politics and tea. She looks up: a weak breeze riffles
the pages on which she has pinned the afternoon

in Indian ink, and their laughter scatters in choked aspen
     trees
where sunlight, regardless, upends both the game
and the ambitions of those plainly put-down words.

Another volume: Spring 1921. The diary laments
they have had a blow: a permit for the motor was refused.
Not so in Ballyturin House, where the tennis party

has broken up in salvered tea and calls for a reprise.
Which might itself have been an entry from the diary,
save for the culminating flourish of bodies, one slumped

over the bonnet like an umpire checking the chalk for dust
or the volley of shots like a flurry of late calls, or the opening
account of play stalled on the lodge gates oddly closed.

After that, it's a holding game, put down to delivery,
service skills, to foot faults or to where advantage falls
and to how often the metaphor is required to work the line

between incident and outrage, between the ins and outs
of the intent or outcome, to the calling out or not in
or only just, to the over and eventual out, out, out.

The Difference

from 'Three Sonnets For Eoin'

Do you remember playing ping-pong?
'It's table-tennis!' you insist:
The white ball hops tick-tock, tick-tock
in garage-walled eternity
where every game's a real cliff-hanger
('let him win!' your mother hisses)
your twenty-one to my nineteen
stage-managed by my greater skill:
too long, too wide, too near the net
we simply can't believe your luck.
You're getting better; you can see
my backhand's useless; soon you'll beat
me fair and square and you won't glean
the difference, but I will.

Tennis in Wicklow

I knew from the way you spooned the ball
Back to me over the sagging net,
Reaching out awkwardly with your racket
And little cries of mock despair,
That you were not an opponent I could live with.

Your sister watched us from the conservatory,
Smoothing down her fringe and throwing words
To a recent victim of her backhand,
Whose short back and sides were just visible
Among the pelargoniums and nerines.

PAUL MULDOON

How to Play Championship Tennis

That winter of my third-form year,
While the other boys played penny poker
Or listened to the latest Hendrix,
Or simply taunted Joe and Cyril,

I fell in with the school caretaker.
He was like me, from the country,
We seemed to speak the same language.
He knew the names of all the trees,

He knew them by their wizened leaves.
Books, too. He had gathered hundreds.
He loved their very smells, their shapes.
There was this book that I might like

That he would give me as a present.
How to Play Championship Tennis.
We would meet the next morning at break
In his little workshop.

The book lay squarely on the table.
I reached for it. But as I stooped
He leaned across and grabbed my pecker.
I ran out by the unkempt lawn

Through a fine, insinuating drizzle.
The net had long been taken down
Yet here were Joe and Cyril, knocking up;
Their fluent lobs, their deft volleys,

As if they had found some other level.

2

Gaelic Football

Footballer

Below in the half-dark,
A boy is hitting a ball against a wall.

Now he races out along the field,
Dancing with it, whispering to it,

As if it were a child or a dog,
As if no world but this existed,

As if this were the world that will exist.

SEAMUS HEANEY

Station Island, VII

I had come to the edge of the water,
soothed by just looking, idling over it
as if it were a clear barometer

or a mirror, when his reflection
did not appear but I sensed a presence
entering into my concentration

on not being concentrated as he spoke
my name. And though I was reluctant
I turned to meet his face and the shock

is still in me at what I saw. His brow
was blown open above the eye and blood
had dried on his neck and cheek. 'Easy now,'

he said, 'it's only me. You've seen men as raw
after a football match ... What time it was
when I was wakened up I still don't know

but I heard this knocking, knocking, and it
scared me, like the phone in the small hours,
so I had the sense not to put on the light

but looked out from behind the curtain.
I saw two customers on the doorstep
and an old Land Rover with the doors open

parked on the street, so I let the curtain drop;
but they must have been waiting for it to move
for they shouted to come down into the shop.

She started to cry then and roll round the bed,
lamenting and lamenting to herself,
not even asking who it was. "Is your head

astray, or what's come over you?" I roared, more
to bring myself to my senses
than out of any real anger at her

for the knocking shook me, the way they kept it up,
and her whingeing and half-screeching made it worse.
All the time they were shouting, "Shop!

Shop!" so I pulled on my shoes and a sportscoat
and went back to the window and called out,
"What do you want? Could you quieten the racket

or I'll not come down at all." "There's a child not well.
Open up and see what you have got – pills
or a powder or something in a bottle,"

one of them said. He stepped back off the footpath
so I could see his face in the streetlamp
and when the other moved I knew them both.

But bad and all as the knocking was, the quiet
hit me worse. She was quiet herself now,
lying dead still, whispering to watch out.

At the bedroom door I switched on the light.
"It's odd they didn't look for a chemist.
Who are they anyway at this hour of the night?"

she asked me, with the eyes standing in her head.
"I know them to see," I said, but something
made me reach and squeeze her hand across the bed

before I went downstairs into the aisle
of the shop. I stood there, going weak
in the legs. I remember the stale smell

of cooked meat or something coming through
as I went to open up. From then on
you know as much about it as I do.'

'Did they say nothing?' 'Nothing. What would they say?'
'Were they in uniform? Not masked in any way?'
'They were barefaced as they would be in the day,

shites thinking they were the be-all and the end-all.'
'Not that it is any consolation,
but they were caught,' I told him, 'and got jail.'

Big-limbed, decent, open-faced, he stood
forgetful of everything now except
whatever was welling up in his spoiled head,

beginning to smile. 'You've put on a bit of weight
since you did your courting in that big Austin
you got the loan of on a Sunday night.'

Through life and death he had hardly aged.
There always was an athlete's cleanliness
shining off him and except for the ravaged

forehead and the blood, he was still that same
rangy midfielder in a blue jersey
and starched pants, the one stylist on the team,

the perfect, clean, unthinkable victim.
'Forgive the way I have lived indifferent –
forgive my timid circumspect involvement,'

I surprised myself by saying. 'Forgive
my eye,' he said, 'all that's above my head.'
And then a stun of pain seemed to go through him

and he trembled like a heatwave and faded.

Munster Football Final 1924

– for Mick O'Connell

from 'That's Football!'

Nothing polarises like a war,
And, of all wars, a civil war is worst;
It takes a century to heal the scars
And even then some names remain accursed.
The tragedies of Kerry, open wounds –
John Joe Sheehy on the run in 'twenty-four,
The Munster Final in the Gaelic Grounds:
There's something more important here than war.
John Joe Sheehy, centre forward, republican,
Con Brosnan, Free State captain, centre-field;
For what they love, they both put down the gun –
On Con's safe conduct, Sheehy takes the field.
In an hour the Kerry team will win.
Sheehy will vanish, on Brosnan's bond, again.

BERNARD O'DONOGHUE

Munster Final

– in memory of Tom Creedon, died 28 August, 1983

The jarveys to the west side of the town
Are robbers to a man, and if you tried
To drive through The Gap, they'd nearly strike you
With their whips. So we parked facing for home
And joined the long troop down the meadowsweet
And woodbine-scented road into the town.
By blue Killarney's lakes and glens to see
The white posts on the green! To be deafened
By the muzzy megaphone of Jimmy Shand
And the testy bray to keep the gangways clear.

As for Tom Creedon, I can see him still,
His back arching casually to field and clear.
'Glory Macroom! Good boy, Tom Creedon!'
We'd be back next year to try our luck in Cork.

We will be back next year, roaring ourselves
Hoarse, praying for better luck. After first Mass
We'll get there early; that's our only hope.
Keep clear of the carparks so we're not hemmed in,
And we'll be home, God willing, for the cows.

Leabharlann
6543434
Contae Na Midhe

NOEL MONAHAN

The Football Field

After the cows are milked, the Old Road comes
Alive on bright evenings. Some tog out in
Cars, I can still hear their studs strut the stones,
Smell the *Wintergreen* on their limbering
Muscles, see them line up in linen-white
Togs, St Mary's blue jerseys, nervously
Awaiting the throw-in:
                    Thump, Thump, Thump …
No surrender until the final whistle blows.
Their feet airborne, fingers claw the clouds,
The ball bounces over humps and hollows,
Forwards dance a can-can, backs are steadfast.
Clabbered in dust and clay about the square,
Hot and bothered, their tempers go haywire.
Their brawls now settled with the dust of years.

SEAMUS HEANEY

The Point

from 'Three Drawings'

Those were the days –
booting a leather football
truer and farther
then you ever expected!

It went rattling
hard and fast
over daisies and benweeds,
it thumped

but it sang too,
a kind of dry, ringing
foreclosure of sound.
Or else, a great catch

and a cry from the touch-line
to *Point her*! That spring
and unhampered smash-through!
Was it you

or the ball that kept going
beyond you, amazingly
higher and higher
and ruefully free?

Minding Goal

One consequence of being stuck
between the netless posts
during hurling practice
was to be guaranteed at least
the task and satisfaction
of hanging the *sliotar* out.

The others clashing and chasing,
jerseyed in various club
and county colours, dreamed
themselves glorious. You squinted
through the oblique sunlight
or pretended the shape of ease,

or crouched, or paced, depending.
A save adorned the goal
opposite, and swiftly the game
turned. Solo-specialist Joe
closed in, all wrist and speed
as he balanced the *sliotar*

on his hurley before swivelling
to lash it past your ear.
What kept you there? Hardly
the prospect of making a save.
And retrieval was a long walk
no-one else would take, a slash

search through lank grass.
Turane Little, Spring twilight –
the losing and the laying claim
both implicit in a sphere
of corded leather tossed up
before your face, and given air.

MICHAEL HARTNETT

Reconstructionists

The GAA decided
the time had come to explain
to very puzzled tourists
the rules of the Hurling Game.
So, as things are quiet in winter,
their decision was to ask
the lads from the Office of Public Works
to help them with their task –
to build an Interpretive Centre;
to unbaffle Icelanders,
Dutchmen, Danes and Turks,
to educate our visitors
and not leave them in the dark,
and to site this latest venture –
where else, but in Croke Park!

The day came for unveiling
and there in snow-white ranks
stood shining sheds of limestone,
with Celtic septic tanks
to service all the toilets
with their sparkling tiles and taps;
and there was a lecture room
hung with very detailed maps
to point the way to Thurles

for Libyans, Letts and Lapps;
and a foyer aglow like the Book of Kells
with an undecipherable graph
that's explained the whole year 'round
by the full-time staff
of two. And for all the lovely money
a Foreign Currency Exchange
clad in gleaming quartz-stone
left over from Newgrange.
And a genuine Irish *siopa té*
with genuine soda bread
made brown with genuine turf dust
to sink in your belly like lead
(one slice of that and, d'you know what,
you'll swear that you've been fed!).

The Fathers of the Nation
rejoiced and they were glad
(the Mother of the Nation
was somewhere west of Chad);
but none of these wise leaders
had foreseen the tiny hitch –
the lads from the Office of Public Works
had built their Temple of Plumbing
in the middle of the pitch!

BRENDAN KENNELLY

The Madness of Football

Beautiful country, driven-out people –
Yakuntya, yahoorya, yabollocksya,
And the boys and the girls studying
For jobs in another country:
   Beautiful country, driven-out people –
I remember Mad Sweeney,
District Inspector Sweeney, to be exact,

Issuing guns in the Phoenix Park
And telling the RIC men
To open fire on the crowds in Croke Park.
Was there a Final feeling that Sunday
Or a totally different kind of sport,
A breakthrough in virile craft and art?
The papers forecast a battle royal.
I stewed in the crowd, I saw men fall.
Beautiful country, driven-out people –
I'm shot through with the madness of football.
Run, hit, kick, score, win. Win. That's all.

A Religious Occasion

I was there for a purpose, not a lark.
I shall long remember
That Sunday afternoon, one mild September,
Standing with 89,374 Catholics in Croke Park

Hearing the Artane Boys' Band play with verve and spark
The National Anthem and *Faith of Our Fathers*.
The Christian faces of the spectators
Were proof of the hard spiritual work

That goes to make true lovers of sport.
I was part of that crowd, one with the electric feeling
That turns a rigid stranger into an instant brother.

It was, dare I say it, a religious occasion.
The ball was thrown in and those two great teams
Proceeded to kick the shit out of each other.

Hay

If the talk of the cap men was music
and they in the half light
half-lit with whiskey,
his voice was the drone,
his chest swelled like bellows, erudite

on anything you'd want to know.
You'd have to think it worry
here and trouble there
to hear his talk of the price of stores,
the damage done by harvest rain, and the sorry

state we're in.
You'd hear blame laid
on governments, on Arabs,
on the weather men, and then he'd moan,
'Sure that's the way. You'll have that, I'm afraid.'

He'd be first at the fair
and last to leave.
He'd kneel at the burying of friends
as a horse stands at the forge,
his weight on one leg, pondering his reprieve

in two parts of a three-piece suit
he cleaned with a currycomb.
He'd find an ally then
to share a lough of drinks.
He'd be in a far place and thinking of home.

At a football final in Croke Park
and the others lost in play
he was staring into the middle distance
of the Hogan Stand and heard himself say,
'Lord it'd hold a world of hay.'

BERNARD O'DONOGHUE

Croke Park or Ballylee, 1989

We propped a bed against the grainloft door
To keep the cats out so the second brood
Of swallows could escape to the power-lines;
But as the end of holiday approached,
We watched more anxiously each day that passed
The swaying, squawking line of them
On the rafters over the cheery birdlime.

We changed the return ferry booking
To extend our guard; and then, one evening
We got back from Galleycove with the sea
Still washing in our ears to find them gone.
Mystery, relief and minor heartache.
They'd left one last decision to be made:
How to spend these extra, God-given days

With the best that Ireland had to offer.
Should we go up to the All-Ireland final,
Or repeat another tried pilgrimage:
The Tarbert ferry, pause at Craggaunowen
To see the Brendan, on past Dysert O'Dea,
And through the Burren to Yeats's Tower
To watch the moorhens from the lancet windows?

It was a question, as we packed the car,
Of which would season better through the nights
Of coming winter: 'they nobbled Tompkins';
'Allen was past it'; or 'you can still see
The winding stair and breathe the mice and damp
Above the starling's nest where "Meditations
In Time of Civil War" was written'.

Look for guidance to the swallows, still
Protesting against ravishment, now from
Their wire-platforms high above the scabious,
Or weaving their telling tapestries
Of air, sticking still to the same story,
Unchanged since last year or last age, after
Their sally from the loft. Here in the uplands

They're safe from the stonechat's mockery
And still the theme of Yeatsian meditation
As they soar away from the old woman's house,
A ruin by a clogged straw tumulus.
In the event we were driving down the bleak
Central plain, straining to hear the commentary
From Dublin above the engine noise.

On a whim we switched it off and turned for Gort,
And walked in Coole Woods, trying to distinguish seven.
We took slips of three rhododendrons and watched
The lake through the mulberry, debating
Uncertainly which was the house and which
The servant's quarters. When we turned on again,
It was just too late to hear the final score.

A Man's World

He could not bear it – a convent funeral,
his female relatives had to chivvy him along.
His cousin Sister Lazarian laid out
in a sky-blue Child of Mary cloak
with a face like a hawk sticking out
of the coffin. The slippery polished floors,
the green crochet-covered bell rope
hanging like a rebuke in the gloom.
He did not go to Mass.
The tapestries, embroidered swans on cushions
pictures of bishops and saints, tea and sandwiches.
There would be *No smoking*.
And yet, the pale eager faces of the nuns –
down the clean corridors the black habits swirled
and skirled. He knew it was party
when the fine white fingers poured Scotch
into a heavy glass right up to the top.
Asking questions about the races,
Tipperary's chances in the All Ireland.
In this purified atmosphere
he was an interesting man
with an interesting smell.
He lit a Sweet Afton and flicked ash
into the hand-held ashtray beside him,
sat back as the coifed and veiled women
arranged themselves around the room
preparing to be mesmerised.

PAUL DURCAN

Sport

There were not many fields
In which you had hopes for me
But sport was one of them.
On my twenty-first birthday
I was selected to play
For Grangegorman Mental Hospital
In an away game
Against Mullingar Mental Hospital.
I was a patient
In B Wing.
You drove all the way down,
Fifty miles,
To Mullingar to stand
On the sidelines and observe me.

I was fearful I would let down
Not only my team but you.
It was Gaelic football.
I was selected as goalkeeper.
There were big country men
On the Mullingar Mental Hospital team,
Men with gapped teeth, red faces,
Oily, frizzy hair, bushy eyebrows.
Their full forward line
Were over six foot tall

Fifteen stone in weight.
All three of them, I was informed,
Cases of schizophrenia.

There was a rumour
That their centre-half forward
Was an alcoholic solicitor
Who, in a lounge bar misunderstanding,
Had castrated his best friend
But that he had no memory of it.
He had meant well – it was said.
His best friend had had to emigrate
To Nigeria.

To my surprise,
I did not flinch in the goals.
I made three or four spectacular saves,
Diving full stretch to turn
A certain goal around the corner,
Leaping high to tip another certain goal
Over the bar for a point.
It was my knowing
That you were standing on the sideline
That gave me the necessary motivation –
That will to die
That is as essential to sportsmen as to artists.

More than anybody it was you
I wanted to mesmerise, and after the game –
Grangegorman Mental Hospital
Having defeated Mullingar Mental Hospital
By 14 goals and 38 points to 3 goals and 10 points –
Sniffing your approval, you shook hands with me.
'Well played, son.'

I may not have been mesmeric
But I had not been mediocre.
In your eyes I had achieved something at last.
On my twenty-first birthday I had played on a winning team
The Grangegorman Mental Hospital team.
Seldom if ever again in your eyes
Was I to rise to these heights.

3
Horse Racing

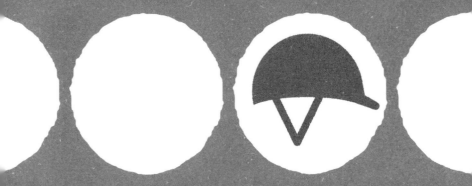

PEGGIE GALLAGHER

The Three Card Trick Man

– after a line by Tom Duddy

The reason I come here is not the horses,
though bookie shops abound and a litter of crushed slips.
It is always sunny and work is over for the weekend
and the girl in the red dress has just stepped out –

not exactly a carnival atmosphere, more
a thoroughfare of anticipation, the mood buoyant,
a painter's delight,
the air still holding the day's warmth.

There he is just off a side-street;
part of a circle hunched around a makeshift table.
The scrubbed nape,
an odour of soap and aftershave.

The picture steadies, the table is swept,
and the look when he turns to her
pales the red of her dress.

Impossible to say what passes between them –
a wager of innocent measure,
the small treacheries of love and its necessities.
Here I will leave them with everything still to play for.

TOM FRENCH

The Race Field

September 11th, low tide

A *Transit* towing a load of furlong markers
whose tracks, the farther it goes, grow fainter.
*

A tractor and a harrow preparing sand
to plant and harvest before the tide turns.
*

On the Race Field gate, that lovely extra *s* –
mulled over and gone with – in *Horses Boxes*.
*

Punters eyeing the horizon, like fishermen;
the fishermen, fishing offshore, study form.
*

Neck and neck on the straight for home,
our hands touch; they have lives of their own.
*

No wind; or no wind worth mentioning;
and still the VIP marquee billowing.
*

He drives the final furlong and digs a hole
that the sea fills, for the final furlong pole.

Laytown Races, 1959

While searching for a place to land
my beloved aviator trails his voice
like a tea stain in the sky.

For he is running dry
across corrugated chalets, open fenlands
and a prairie of saline fields.

He wonders how far above the tide mark
we should stake out his course
while reeling in a line of stage fright

and, though the radio has no report of this,
I see the shy heat of the dunes,
the beach becoming crowded

and men strolling down Tiernan's Lane.
Why then should my mother say,
in thrall to the turning of the year –

he will come from the marsh road
past the links and the bawn?
For decked out in khaki

I'll soon be called to eat or swim.
The horses are held back with bunting.
A languorous tide is coming in.

Gowran Park,
Autumn Meeting

The year's potatoes, they've ploughed them out,
The threshing rig's gone round about;
Earth finishes with the harvest time.

A low sun noses through the damps;
The trees are bare down to the stumps;
A mist can spring up white as lime.

The fox is red as the huntsman's coat,
The doublebarrel rhymes a note,
The season turns on the hill;

But day sits up like a hunkered hare
As horse and jockey catch the roar;
Gowran lights like a paper spill.

Soon long shadows will creep from the grill
Of every gate, the mountains stamp,
The year fall into the Christmas lamp.

W . B . Y E A T S

At Galway Races

There where the course is,
Delight makes all of the one mind,
The riders upon the galloping horses,
The crowd that closes in behind:
We, too, had good attendance once,
Hearers and hearteners of the work;
Aye, horsemen for companions,
Before the merchant and the clerk
Breathed on the world with timid breath.
Sing on: somewhere at some new moon,
We'll learn that sleeping is not death,
Hearing the whole earth change its tune,
Its flesh being wild, and it again
Crying aloud as the racecourse is,
And we find hearteners among men
That ride upon horses.

TOM DUDDY

The Racing Festival

The reason I come here is not the horses
(a rumble and outcry on the horizon)
but these carnival odours of plastic
and bruised grass; and the hawkers' bric-a-brac

of water rifles, tea-sets, cap guns, dolls,
foot-pumps, and hammers with slender handles;
and the Wheel of Fortune and other tricky sports
with rings, cards, darts, and tickets rolled in straws.

Here nothing is guaranteed; there is no value
for money; the hammer will snap in two
at the first attempt to crack a hazelnut
on the hearthstone; the gauge will soon twist

off the blue foot-pump. The youngest kids
no longer know what the hell a cap gun is
and wouldn't be seen dead in hard little stetsons;
the Wheel of Fortune man is impersonal

and sullen, wiping the coins off his reds
and blacks, as if they were his by rights.
Here among cheap jacks and trick-o-the-loopers,
among these winners poorer than losers

I am elated, light hearted, beside myself.

Action Replays

– for my brother Seamus

1.

Tired of ice, the flawed mintage
chipped from our buckets,
drips spiking the eaves,

we take to the snowfields,
cantering on the trail
of a jockey named Winter.

Chepstow and Market Rasen
run in our heads,
the sound of Wincanton:

racecourse England,
its thunderous afternoons
of furlongs and fences.

We are the 3.30, a two-horse race
through Donnelly's Bottom.
When we lap

the 4 o'clock, already our sights are set
on the 4.40 before darkness falls,
the next stumbling freeze.

2.

That day you stumbled off the scaffolding,
you fell with a jockey's instinct, rolling clear,
remounted. The dark stayer timing its run
that trailed our father thirty years before
took ten days to catch you.
                              Now you walk
the backroads, day in day out, as though to stop
might ground you forever:
                              I flog the tired horse
of old endeavours, dreaming it might yet clear
your memory's blurred fences or, bolting, alarm
the least twitch in the nerves of a dead arm.

Lone Patrol

You told me about him. The small horse
is one of your memories, the few
remaining, a barrel of a two-year-old
who burned himself on your inner eye
in the '40s and never left, galloping round
the inside track of broken recall,
a colt crouching under a ditch by the Bride
for two winters, then racing, unbeaten
in bumpers, over hurdles, over fences
with Sean Hyde on his back, a Rapparee
ranging over the rough courses of the South
in the days when horses were bought
and sold for a song. Your father paid
a Mrs Watt for him in the Grand Hotel
and there he was. Tramore, Listowel
Limerick Junction, you with your father,
your main man, the two of you travelling
the race meetings of Munster together –
you will never forget him –
the rough and ready days of mud,
three-card-tricksters and tic-tac men,
and you making a book with your father
in the rain, always the rain. Lone Patrol –
sent to England in the end, there was no
future for him here, the stocky body

weaving in the sharp bends, the low frame
steady in the home strait, lone scout
holding the line, but too small
for the steeplechase at Market Rasen.
He broke his back, the sentinel
who still patrols your lonesome fens
and borderlands.

F.R. HIGGINS

The Old Jockey

His last days linger in that low attic
That barely lets out the night,
With its gabled window on Knackers' Alley,
Just hoodwinking the light.

He comes and goes by that gabled window
And then on the window-pane
He leans, as thin as a bottled shadow –
A look and he's gone again:

Eyeing, maybe, some fine fish-women
In the best shawls of the Coombe
Or, maybe, the knife-grinder plying his treadle,
A run of sparks from his thumb!

But, O you should see his gazing, gazing,
When solemnly out on the road
The horse-drays pass overladen with grasses,
Each driver lost in his load;

Gazing until they return; and suddenly,
As galloping by they race,
From his pale eyes, like glass breaking,
Light leaps on his face.

The Wide World

He loves racing,
Cheltenham, Ascot,
Leopardstown, Mallow,
Newmarket, Tralee
and Galway.

I like it here.
The kitchen smell.
Quiet. Peppers, apple.
The kitchen table
scored with lines
from my knife.

Garlic, fennel, onions.

When we first met
the sky was blue flames
over Montenotte.

Now I like feeling rested,
waking up when the morning
is not spoilt. Paperbacks propped
against saucepans, no rain
inside my collar or shoe.

Potato, tomato, thyme.

I could have gone
to the races too.
Risked the blue flames,
the comets,
the hangovers.

Kentucky, bluegrass, racing.

4

Golf, Pitch & Putt

MATTHEW SWEENEY

The Yellow Golf Ball
on the Lawn

Every time I come in the gate, I see it
lurking in the grass, beside the bio bin.
And I ask myself how it got here. We
are so far from any golf course, that no
golfer, however long-hitting, could loft
a ball that far. Could a dog have brought it?
I've never seen a dog invader, only
cats, and they wouldn't touch a golf ball.
Crows' beaks don't open wide enough,
nor even seagulls'. No, it has to be human –
but who? My neighbours are not golfers.
I know because I was one myself,
a long time ago, elsewhere, but still –
we walk in a certain way, hesitate
before making moves, take our bearings
from the sun, test the wind. Could it be
that I might have brought that ball here?

I lost many a golf ball when younger,
and once or twice they were yellow.
Not often, but I did try them sometimes.
And I remember the mysterious vanishing
of a yellow ball, when I was in danger
of winning a competition. We searched,
and searched, in vain. I had to add the

two penalty strokes, and lost, of course.
Could this be that ball – flown all the way
from Donegal to Cork, through four
decades, to lie there waiting for my shot?
But where is the flag and the green, and
more pertinently, where are my clubs?
What am I supposed to do – kick it?
Grab a gardening trowel and bury it?
Or should I pick the ball up tomorrow,
pocket it, and drop it in the River Lee?

MAURICE RIORDAN

He Begins with a
Line by Sandy Lyle

from 'Mediums'

There's more to life than hitting a golf ball
and more to life than this bitch the farming life,
more to it than lying in a hammock at Bill Duffy's farm.
There's more to life than wasting one's life,
though there's more life in wasters than you'd think.
Though it's more thinking what life is like
than it is the thing itself.
For the thing about life is it's crazier and more of it than
     you think.
And the more there is the more we want
and what we want we live to regret,
for what one wants one gets too late or spends too quick.
Getting and regretting we lay waste our powers,
and it is the waste remains and kills.
One could do worse than lay in a hammock all one's life,
and take up late in life the game of golf.

CONOR O'CALLAGHAN

Pitch & Putt

Its is the realm of men
and boys joined in boredom,
the way of life that sees
one day on a par
with the next and school breaks
dragged out too long.

Theirs is the hour killed slowly,
the turn for home
in diminishing threes and twos,
the provisional etiquette
of shared tees,
conceded defeat.

Theirs the loose end,
the nationality of ships
in the absence
of shop to talk,
the freedom to be hopeless
and still come back.

Theirs the blather
of the last twoball
accepting flukes
for what they are,
the greenkeeper collecting flags
and shadows in their wake.

DAVID WHEATLEY

Moonshine

The ball dribbles off the green and into the drink.
My round at Druid's Glen isn't going too well.
A man in ridiculous trousers eyes up a putt.
Afterwards there will be G & Ts all round.

⋆

My great-grandfather, the steward, is doing the rounds
on the Tottenham estate, the golf-course-to-be. Should he put
up a fence around it or brick up the old well
lest anyone fall down it into the drink?

⋆

It's years now since the place was sold. They did well
out of it too, I was told once over a drink
by a Tottenham cousin of theirs (I get around)
who told me another story he had off pat:

⋆

how an ancestor whose body was covered in weals,
poor man, lived on the same estate and used to put
wine in his bath, which his wily steward drained,
bottled and sold for the unwitting locals to drink.

JOHN O'DONNELL

Poetry

– for Conor O'Callaghan

The dark nights at the driving range.
The early starts, sun singing off the dew.
The shudder, standing up to open ground
On the first tee. The many ways of being wrong:
Hooked. Sliced. Topped. Shanked. Pulled.
The floundering for hours in bunkers
And still not getting out. The lost balls.
The prizes everyone else wins. The drinking.
The yardage, working out how far to go.
The ones that start off looking great but end up
Short. The shots that try to do too much. The know-alls.
The two-foot putts that you still miss. The yips.
And – sometimes – the little click when things go right:
The sweet sound that keeps you coming back.

Remembering Certain Golf Holes

– for Roger

Most are forgotten before you reach the next tee.
Encounters, not as brief as they might have been:
A mixed-bag of drives, chips and scrambled bogeys.

But certain holes resurface in your mind at night:
That stillness at the pitch of a perfect swing,
Rushes and swamp, trees split by shafting light

As pussy willow billows wild in some ditch.
The instant when a white ball soared or rolled
And life elsewhere momentarily ceased to exist.

Often you lie awake, longing to replay some shot
With what semblance of sense you've since picked up.
But you would happily repeat every single mistake

For the time your shot carried the lake and furze
Onto a fairway curving past trees placed to punish
Any golfer who avoided taking on the nest of bunkers.

You watched your ball rise, like a starling taking fright,
To get lost against the blueness of an evening skyline,
Where you were lost too, bewitched by the arc of its flight.

5

Handball & Bowls

Squarings, XI

To put a glass roof on the handball alley
Where a hopped ball cut merciless angles
In and out of play, or levelled true

For the unanswerable dead-root ...
He alone, our walking weathercock,
Our peeled eye at the easel, had the right

To make a studio of that free maze,
To turn light outside in and curb the space
Where accident got tricked to accuracy

And rain was rainier for being blown
Across the grid and texture of the concrete.
He scales the world at arm's length, gives thumbs up.

Handball Legend

Outside the church I heard bits and pieces.
Someone told the story of Jarlath's last day,
how he'd left his sister's house and walked

two miles to the golf course in his pyjamas.
He'd been in bed all the previous month,
her feeding him a bottle a day, no questions.

Someone on the fifth tee had seen Jarlath searching
for balls in the drain off the second fairway.
'He would have done that a lot as a boy,'

someone else said respectfully. 'A golf ball
is a great tool for a hard-as-nails handballer.
Toughens the hands.' The coffin appeared then,

six massive grey brothers bearing it, all of them
weeping. We blessed ourselves, and someone said,
softly, 'Makes *shite* of the hands, more like.'

GREG DELANTY

After Viewing *The Bowling Match at Castlemary, Cloyne, 1847*

I promised to show you the bowlers
    out the Blarney Road after Sunday mass,
you were so taken with that painting
    of the snazzy, top-hatted peasant class
        all agog at the bowler in full swing,
        down to his open shirt, in trousers
as indecently tight as a baseballer's.

You would relish each fling's span
    along blackberry boreens, and delight
in a dinger of a curve throw
    as the bowl hurls out of sight,
        not to mention the earthy lingo
        & antics of gambling fans,
giving players thumbs-up or down the banks.

It's not just to witness such shenanigans
    for themselves, but to be relieved
from whatever lurks in our background,
    just as the picture's crowd is freed
        of famine & exile darkening the land,
        waiting to see where the bowl spins
off, a planet out of orbit, and who wins.

6
Soccer

Manager, Perhaps

The first time I met Oliver Cromwell
The poor man was visibly distressed.
'Buffún' says he, 'things are gone to the devil
In England. So I popped over here for a rest.
Say what you will about Ireland, where on
Earth could a harassed statesman find peace like
This in green unperturbed oblivion?
Good Lord! I'm worn out from intrigue and work.
I'd like a little estate down in Kerry,
A spot of salmon-fishing, riding to hounds.
Good Lord! The very thought makes me delighted.
Being a sporting chap, I'd really love to
Get behind one of the best sides in the land.
Manager, perhaps, of Drogheda United?'

ROBERT GREACEN

Goals

A street singer is droning:
'You are all I have, sonny boy.'
Al Jolson reigns OK.
Corner boys scuffle like sparrows
As they pitch and toss for pennies.
Cigarette smoke blues the twilight
Eddies off to the shipyard.
A boy, messenger of the gods,
Lithe Mercury in uniform,
Dashes past on a red bicycle,
Telegram in his pouch,
Drama in a dozen words.

I clasp a football reeking of leather.
I'm captain, Willie's centre-forward,
Our jackets mark the goalposts.
We scramble over cobbles, graze knees,
Get shouted at by a housewife
Anxious for her glossy windows.
The lamplighter with his pole
Startles the mantles into life,
Gaslight signals our end-game.
The ball bounces towards a magnetic field,
Goal on dream goal
And the victor's wreath
Lures us to great Saturdays,
Thunder on the terraces.

DAVID PARK

George Best

Once I tried to pin him to the page
Tackle him with the heaviness of words
But with a sudden drop of one shoulder
And a slight shimmy of hips he was gone,
Leaving me stumbling off balance,
The page a withering wake of empty space,
His heels disappearing into the distance
Like some skipping dance of trickster light.

MIRIAM GAMBLE

Tinkerness

– in memory of George Best

Something in the way you man that ball
is endemic to this city.
As you spoon it down the field
you are both barbarian and ballet-
girl: as rough and ready as they come, with a zing
that's ever-so-slightly off the mark.
I can almost hear you saying:
'That thing's as hard as a hoor's heart'
to the notion that something might be fragile,
the injunction to take care
as you blaze seamlessly from goal to goal,
and, latterly, disaster to disaster,
taking life one dance-step at a time,
never thinking about the future, each move
an explosion of your love. A love,

perhaps, that also carried, even in its prime,
a fair share of that 'drug-dull fatalism' ascribed to us:
that had taken from the red-brick terraces of east
Belfast more than anyone could fathom
from the flick of your fleet feet. Snow looms
in the grey sky of your maiden city on this cold
November afternoon, and they interrupt the run of the radio
as you have always interrupted plans,
diving in when you were least expected,

a blur of energy kitted out in black and white and red.
You were the fierce alembic of your homeland,
your dream-runs down and around Cregagh Road
going on to render you ambassador, to wide worlds,
of a certain sideways motion: the last perverse twist;
quips tailor-made in this city of oddments.

ELAINE FEENEY

Ryan Giggs is a Ride

– for Jack

1.

I stuck Ryan Giggs pictures
on my blue walls,
down on the skirting boards,
match stickers
all over my wardrobe
and on my window sill.

I stuck Ryan Giggs letters
in the green post-box
on the corner of
Court Lane and High Street,

like a desperate pyrotechnic lover.

I begged him to love me so
I stuck in the language of Shakespeare.

I should have
turned up at his door
and asked him for a ride.

Or married his brother.

I wasted lots of paper.

Then we lost contact.

I started wearing
black crushed velvet
and smoking pot.

I started biting my nails hard
and chasing boys with
back issues of *X-Men*.

    2.

I married a Liverpool fan
I have a son who wants to be a Liverpool player
I have a son who wants to be a tree

And I stick their photos all
over my side of the bed,
and all down the skirting board,
they're all over our old
paraná pine wardrobe
and even frescoes
on the window-sill,

just for when the
transfer market opens –
and I lose one of them.

The Beautiful Game

Sunday afternoon in August, sunny, warm,
Watching TV – the beautiful game
Being played with professional ugliness,
Manchester United versus Aston Villa.
My floor littered with the customary Sabbath garbage:
Newspapers, newspapers, more newspapers.

Such a tender knock on the door, I wonder –
Did I imagine it?
I unlock it and see before me
A handsome, middle-aged woman
In dull gold tank-top, dull gold slacks.
I have never seen her before in my life.

I peer out at her over my reading specs,
Not knowing what to say to her,
Saying 'Yes?'
She does not speak, but returns
My perplexed, anxious gaze.
She says: 'Nessa.'

'Oh Nessa!'
We'd been married for fifteen years
A long time ago.
I switch off the TV,

Interrupting
The beautiful game.

'I am on my way back to Cork.'
Twenty minutes later she resumes her journey,
Driving away in her blue machine.
I do not switch back on the TV.
I have had more than enough,
For one afternoon, of the beautiful game.

ALAN GILLIS

If There was Time
All Day to Wait

– in memory of Jim Kelly

Not a minute has passed. If only it was time
to quit, to leave the desk and screen with all
their clocks. You've double-checked the time
for the fifteenth time
in the last ten minutes. If only the day
would clear the scowl of its sky sometime
soon you might find the time
to take a turn about. If she could come too.
If only Harry Kewell could get back to
the form of his prime, his time
at Leeds, before burdened with the weight
of expectation. It's a heavyweight

punch to the whatnots to be made to wait
to no end. If there was money enough, then time
would be no worry. Take the weight
off your feet. But the day's a dead weight
and in your ear you always hear the call
of the future: 'Delayed. Please wait
in queue.' So shuffle your pens and paperweight,
double-check the weather. And what a day
for the Big Man to finally say: 'Today
we have begun to plant and we await
the harvest.' Was that it? The temperature is fair to
middling but the clouds are too

heavy for high hope. Gerrard will have to
play a stormer, carry the weight
of everyone; and everyone will be up to
high do when they hear. Someone should say to
the Big Man: 'Hallelujah. Amen, and about time
too. But what was wrong in '69 or '72?'
Too bad for everyone who's had to
bear him out, too bad for – what did he call
them? – the honoured and unageing dead, for all
that tomorrow is to-
morrow and this, as he says, is today.
AC Milan looked the business last Wednesday.

You heard him rasp and roil one Sunday
by the City Hall, his head raised to
the heavens haranguing shoppers with Doomsday.
Now he says we know not what a day
may bring forth. Back then, he couldn't wait
for those clouds to burst. A new day.
Well, bring it on. A tumour as broad as the day
is long. A time to break down and a time
to build up; a time to keep and a time
to get blootered and blather at the end of the day,
singing 'You'll Never Walk Alone' all
alone, ripping it out, for once and for all.

If only we had another Rush or Fowler, an all-
out finisher who'd prey the entire match-day
for a match-winning through-ball.
Who'd never waver if a chance should fall.
Happiness, his good book says, will come to
him who rewards his enemies as they all
have served him. Which, you thought, meant bugger all
but trouble until now. Thrown like pennyweights
against the rocks of his rage. The deadweight
of his history. If she could phone with the all-
clear you could make the train in time
to walk through the park: arrange a time

to meet her by the gate, and take your time
to walk through the gardens, as if you'd all
the time in the world. For the day
has surely come when there's nothing to
do but get on with it. You can't wait.

– 8 May 2007

Ireland Is Changing Mother

Don't throw out the loaves
with the dishes mother.
It's not the double-takes so much
it's that they take you by the double.
And where have all the Nellys gone
and all the Missus Kellys gone?
You might have had
the cleanest step on your street
but so what mother,
nowadays it's not the step
but the mile that matters.

Meanwhile the Bally Bane Taliban
are battling it out over that football.
They will bring the local yokels
to a deeper meaning of over the barring it.
And then some scarring will occur –
as in cracked skull for your troubles.
They don't just integrate, they *limp-pa-grate*,
your sons are shrinking mother.

Before this mother,
your sons were Gods of that powerful thing.
Gods of the apron string.
They could eat a horse and they often did,

with your help mother.
Even Tim who has a black belt in sleepwalking
and border lining couldn't torch a cigarette,
much less the wet haystack of desire,
even he can see, Ireland is changing mother.
Listen to black belt Tim mother.

When they breeze onto the pitch
like some Namibian Gods
the local girls wet themselves.
They say in a hurry, O-Ma-God, O-Ma-God!

Not good for your sons mother,
who claim to have invented everything
from the earwig to the *sliotar*.
They were used to seizing Cynthia's hips
looking into her eyes and saying
I'm Johnny come lately, love me.

Now the Namibian Gods and the Bally Bane Taliban
are bringing the local yokels
to their menacing senses,
and scoring more goals than Cú Chulainn.
Ireland is changing mother
tell yourself, tell your sons.

Soccer Moms

They remember Gene Chandler topping the charts with
    'Duke of Earl'
when the boys were set on taking the milk bar's one
    banquette
and winning their hearts, Mavis and Merle,

as it seemed their hearts might be first to yield,
hearts before minds. Time for stilettos. Time for spivs
    with shivs.
The time of day when light fails on the field

while their daughters, themselves now tweenie girls,
crowd round a coach for one last tête-à-tête.
They remember Gene Chandler topping the charts with
    'Duke of Earl'

while the world still reeled
from the anti-Castro Cubans going to sea in a sieve,
as it seemed. Their hearts might be first to yield

if only after forty years of one plain, one purl,
on the sweater they've sweated over for a Bay of Pigs vet,
and winning their hearts, Mavis and Merle,

may now be faintly likelier for a well-heeled
schlub to whom they once wouldn't so much as give
the time of day. When light fails on the field

a schlubster linesman will unfurl
an offside flag that signals some vague threat,
they remember. Gene Chandler topping the charts with
    'Duke of Earl'

for three weeks only in 1962 might have taught them to
    shield
themselves against the lives their daughters briefly relive,
as it seemed *their* hearts might be first to yield

to this free kick that forever curls
past the goal-mouth, a ball at once winging into the back
    of the net
and winning. Their hearts, Mavis and Merle,

hanker for the time when it was not yet revealed
failure's no less literal than figurative,
the time of day when light fails on the field

and gives back a sky more muddy than mother-of-pearl,
so it's with a deepening sense of regret
they remember Gene Chandler topping the charts with
    'Duke of Earl'
and winning their hearts, Mavis and Merle.

The Fathers Raising the Nets for the Last Game of the Season: a Triptych

In the opening panel, in the mouth of the container
where the club stores its nets, the fathers who rose
early to help – two bearing the bundle of a net each
in their arms; another, the corner flags; two more,
short steps and the pins cut from reinforcing rods.

In the main panel, the first net is half up. Four fathers
are on their knees like gleaners as the guarded harvest
is carted to the quays, taking the slack back up under
the ground bar and tying, with slip knots, the ties.

Half of the crossbar clips are clipped, (the uprights
have been done already by the shorter men);
Jeff is at full stretch on the steps, one hand grasping
the crossbar to steady himself, the other stretching
for the next clip, (even though his son has been out

with a hamstring for most of the season). One of
the Eastern European dads, holding the hammer
down by his side as if to get the blood to flow back
to his hand, who would pass for a centurion, will
sink the two pins when Jeff has the last clip in.

Then there's just the cord to be tied to the green
uprights behind that lift the net and give it that clean,
square look, and make it tremble when a cross, struck
sweetly from distance and at speed, slams home.
Now the beginning is over. It is all about to begin.

In this, the final panel, the boys are carrying each other.
One wears the lid of a silver trophy on his head. They have
never known such joy. Receding, in the background,
two bundles – too low to be clouds, yet far enough away –
are being borne by the dads who slept later, yet still came.

They will come again, when they've put this summer
behind them, and feel grateful again for these nets,
without which they would be men in the midst of grass
bellowing *'House! House! House!'* where no house is,
at sons running to forestall what is bound to happen next.

7
Running

JOHN O'DONNELL

Sports Day

Suburban pastoral, this: off-white sky,
desultory screech of tannoy; medalled
winners in a swoon of bliss. Her new
partner in tow, the red-nailed mother glides
past paunchy dads consoling flat-foot sons

who'll later cheer them in the Father's Race
as they lollop puff-cheeked towards the line,
the near-seizure worth it to save face. End of term;
loss thickens in the air, in stifled classrooms,
empty; *what now* whisper the corridors, the stairs

What now? The egg-and-spoon
of marriage? The workplace tug-of-war?
Outside at the finish, *sturm und drang;*
the hundred metres is close-run. For every boy
breasting the tape there are, will be

so many also-rans, who'll prise open
the future's oyster-shell to find a world
of sand instead of pearl. How they
clamour as they line up, eager at the start,
flush-faced and staring down the track

as if it were the barrel of a gun,
listening for the starting-pistol's crack
that sends them scampering away
from all of this, bright rags of colour
streaming out into a dying sun.

THEO DORGAN

Running with the Immortals

Cobh is a world of silence as the sun breaks over the harbour
and the lighthouse at Roche's Point gleams, a torch
held out to the sky, to the eternal sea.
Something has woken me early, a drum tap, footfall echoing
in the empty streets. I'm at the open window. Too late –
    whoever it is
has already gone by, climbing the hill, steady and sure.

A clear mid-winter morning, frost on the slate beneath me,
tumble of roof and chimney down to the water. Already
the ferry tracking out towards Haulbowline, the world
    about its business
at this ungodly hour – and someone out there running
    the steep
blue streets. Hard work. Cobh is nothing if not uphill
and downhill, the uphill and downhill capital of Ireland.

On a morning like this, a girlchild out early would be
    thinking of glory –
the tall bowl of the stadium, black roar of the crowd, the
    red track,
the bend to the straight, the finish just visible through
    the haze.
Easy to dream of gold, olive-wreath, ceremony and applause,
the tricolour snapping to the arc-lights overhead, brass
    blaze of trumpets

– harder to rise to these winter mornings, these
    punishing hills,

yet somebody's up and out there, out there unseen and
    unknown,
climbing and falling with the street, breath raw in her throat,
pushing towards the sun, pushing against a wall of cold.
Bells from the Cathedral break over the waking town
while she keeps running on self-belief into the dawn,
an ordinary girl, head down, keeping time with her shadow.

I turn my face to the climbing sun, remembering
    another world,
a tall girl surging to the line. I want to find that child's soul
    and say:
Talent is not enough, belief is not enough in this world;
you must push out into the lonely place where it all
    falls away –
and then, if you're lucky and blessed, the friend at your
    shoulder,
keeping pace, will be long-legged clear-eyed Artemis herself.

Great North

Although we may have bolted from that sad cliff
of our imminent decline, we are not Paula Radcliffe.

And though we may have startled
at the starting pistol,

with its jolt
of explosive (fired by Sting), Usain Bolt

we are not,
by a long shot.

And even though we purchased the slim new book he
called *What I Talk About When I Talk About Running*, we are
        not Haruki

Murakami,
most definitely

not. Wired to our iPods,
We are your average, middle-aged bipeds:

half-trained, stiff-hinged, pegging up the course,
as likely overtaken by a pantomime horse

as a Lady Gaga … In the name of God!
In the name of a small but worthy charity, we plod

on, to the finish and vitality,
fleeing those intimations of mortality.

Keeping in Shape

– for Liam O'Callaghan

'Room for two more?'
I wheeze at the gravedigger
as we jog heavily
past the graveyard.

'Two and more,'
he replies,
loudly, heartily, eternally.

8
Cycling

VINCENT WOODS

Bicycle

from 'Thirteen Acres'

It is 1932, early June, a girl of twelve
has a brand new bicycle, shining black,
the neighbours (some of them) are jealous:
look at her Mary Curley riding a bicycle
before she can crawl and where did they
get the money anyway? Must be that aunt
Kate home from America and making a show
of herself learning to ride a bike at her age,
she'll hardly need wheels in New York, now;
not on a pram anyway, that must be colour
in her hair, too red to be natural, next thing
they'll have a radio, and wait till you see her
at the bonfire, airs and graces, though it's
debatable could she afford a bicycle at all
if all her money went in the Crash three years
ago; and what will become of that young one,
brains to burn and cycling around the roads
like she was a lady of leisure when there's
six more to her heels and for all they bought
her a bike they can't afford an education:
though she'll have education enough up in Coyle's,
as well she's strong, she'll need to be.

And Mary, free for a summer, glides the roads,
the giddy hills, lake speeding past, blue sky
to her shoulder, naming each house, each thatch
and slate, each family. Filled with life, her hair
a pale flame in the wind, past meadows
and men working, stream down the dip at Curraghs
and this is how a girl can fly, who could be happier
than now? And on the cobbled street of home, her
sheepdog, eyes aglint, Aunt Kate in the doorway,
impatient to cycle sedate to the Galley bridge and back,
her mother at the dam of water, two silver buckets
in her hands.

LOUIS MACNEICE

The Cyclist

Freewheeling down the escarpment past the unpassing horse
Blazoned in chalk the wind he causes in passing
Cools the sweat of his neck, making him one with the sky,
In the heat of the handlebars he grasps the summer
Being a boy and to-day a parenthesis
Between the horizon's brackets; the main sentence
Waits to be picked up later but these five minutes
Are all to-day and summer. The dragonfly
Rises without take-off, horizontal,
Underlining itself in the sliver of peacock light.

And glaring, glaring white
The horse on the down moves within his brackets,
The grass boils with grasshoppers, a pebble
Scutters from under the wheel and all this country
Is spattered white with boys riding their heat-wave,
Feet on a narrow plank and hair thrown back

And a surf of dust beneath them. Summer, summer –
They chase it with butterfly nets or strike it into the deep
In a little red ball or gulp it lathered with cream
Or drink it through closed eyelids; until the bell
Left-right-left gives his forgotten sentence
And reaching the valley the boy must pedal again
Left-right-left but meanwhile

For ten seconds more can move as the horse in the chalk
Moves unbeginningly calmly
Calmly regardless of tenses and final clauses
Calmly unendingly moves.

–July 1946

JOHN F. DEANE

Bikes

At the crossroads a big, joint-squealing gate
leads from the back yard to the road, an opening
out from the known world. Neighbours came
to leave their high-framed dray-horse bikes
slouched to the wall inside the gate, and took the bus
to their destinations. We assumed free rein
and took to pedalling round the yard, the bikes
bucking like jittery donkeys at our hands. But oh
how we raced, wee riders, relishing all the while
a watchful guilt, a boldness always on the point
of tears at a gashed knee or a sideways fall
into a tangle of chain and handlebars. We earned
accumulated secrecies when the travellers returned
puzzled at fine-groomed bikes standing to attention.

Fishing, Archery, Falconry & Skiing

Two Brothers Up

Morning. Fifteen books beside a window,
palimpsest of last year's pen upon a table,
ten good fingers to take Propertius down,
ten small winds to enter by the window-glass.

Again, little brother, you appear below,
a fishing-rod flicks above your shoulder.
The hooks in your hand see brown trout leaping
and a sliding heap between trees and water.

Your arm is raised in valediction,
white and small beside the forest.
Tracks go metalled, but never a carriage.
A strand of berries across the track:

your sudden stick takes blood for morning.
Brick wall, stone wall, walks the forest.
A hundred trees, a thousand, a hundred,
come up thick from the yearless clay.

Your boots disturb and brown the river.
Leaves boat down the trouted water.
Sun falls whitely. Propertius talks:
a stream, a god, another autumn.

PATRICK DEELEY

Fisherman

He seems to have set his gaze
on night descending above the Dodder wall
against which he is leaning.

There is nothing, his whole demeanour
says, need fuss him either side,
road or river, not even the rod

which he will almost as a gesture of homage
lift, once in a while, towards
the white willow holding the far bank.

Again he'll cast, always without looking,
in token acknowledgement, perhaps,
of the breeze or a heron's

silent passing. He can't be taken
as fishing for anything. He is all disinterest.
The cigarette dangling from his lip

has some time ago gone out. When
a moth plops into the water,
its belly-flop breaking the silver skin, he

hasn't heard, he will not look.
Then a flicker of trout, a splashing high tail.
He doesn't know, being lost,

apparently, in currents of lamplight
or in his own flow. And just as not much of
anything makes you want to watch

any further, he's turned into the sudden
tugging on his hand and eye,
who now, without to do, will land the fish.

Finding the Ox

A Zen warrior searches for inner peace.
His bow is like a harp, that he might twang its string
In lonely combat with himself, and so release
The arrow of desire. An archer should want nothing.

His is the blue music of what is happening.
His sword rings true. Its many lives of hammered steel
Were there before him, and he trusts its weighty swing.
He knows the rallentando of a roulette wheel,

Or red leaves floating in a stream of eau de nil,
Bisected by a showy rival blade, while his
The leaves avoided. He's the opposite of zeal.

When he aims at the bull he closes his eyes.
Sometimes he hits it dead-on with a mighty whizz.
Sometimes he's way off target, which is no surprise.

The Curée

from 'A Quartet For The Falcon'

The secretive hart turns at bay,
lowers his tines to the hounds' cry.
The sword enters the bull's heart –
             still he stands,
      amazed on the red sand
as the stony unbeliever might,

who has seen God. Soon now
horns will sound *dedow*
for the unmaking. Beaters flush
           the grey heron
      like a coney from its warren,
the peregrine's jet eyes flash.

They go ringing up the air,
each in its separate spiral stair
to the indigo rim of the skies,
           then descend
      swift as a murderer's hand
with a knife. Death's gesture liquefies

in bringing the priestly heron down.
Her prize, the marrow from a wing-bone
in which she delights, her spurred
                    fleur-de-lys tongue
        stained *gold-vermilion* –
little angel in her hangman's hood.

Seeing Things

At the Winter Park ski-holiday reunion
who swans in only Stevie
whose legs don't take him far –
he'd been tinkering under a car
when the bomb went off.

Answer: the skin.
It's Trivia night
and we're in with a chance.
All the other tables are offering liver.
What is the largest organ in the body?

In Winter Park we're triple-
wrapped in thermals
but he's shirtless:
a sophisticated instrument
of thermo-regulation.

Homeostasis: the body
as a furnace;
the sweat-glands
and erector pili muscles
co-operate to keep the body cool.

The hypothalamus
is conductor of the body's
secret business;

but skin grafts don't have glands
and scars are bald.

Anyway Stevie has walked
the twenty yards from his special car
and he's wrecked
and his stumps are sore
and we get tore in to the drink

and we all get legless
and everyone in the Welly Bar
(we're only here for the ramps
and we've jumped the queue)
is legless and Stevie has taken his off,

all smooth American tan
with the socks and the cool shoes on,
and we laugh out loud
at the pretty woman
on stilts who almost

jumps out of her skin
and the plastered people
who swear
they're seeing things
and we know they are.

Indoor / Outdoor Sports & Games

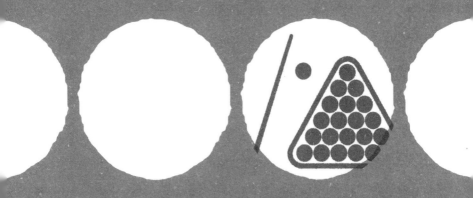

Green Baize Couplets

1.

A handshake, a lowered light, the chance to clear her table
with what at first glance would appear to be a natural
    double.

2.

Her colours on their spots, the cue-ball positioned
    perfectly …
Under normal circumstances, this would be a formality.

3.

Still she rattles on. What I would give for a referee's voice
to bellow from the shadows an authoritative 'Quiet, please.'

4.

A consummate technician, with one eye on the score,
intent on not over-reaching, keeping one foot on the floor.

5.

Fallen beyond arm's length, I begin to feel the tension,
throw my eyes to heaven, and ask for the extension.

6.

A sip of something on ice, having left it in the jaws,
to the horror of yours truly, the absence of applause.

7.

After her kiss on the green, my unexpected cannon,
we go to the mid-session interval with honours pretty
much even.

8.

A hint of gentle side, a couple of messed-up plants,
a kick, a longish pink, and the glimpse of a second chance.

9.

However long it takes, we'll continue this black ball fight
though by now the heat is off and the meter has run out.

10.

Just as you join us, she has given me a shot to nothing,
and I am about to reply by pinning her to the cushion.

PAUL DURCAN

The 2003 World Snooker Championship

Don't lecture me about lint on the baize –
I am ninety-six years of age.

What an old woman like me needs
More than a meal or medicine
Or a life sentence in a nursing home
Is seventeen days in front of the television
In my own home
Watching the World Snooker Championship
In the Crucible in Sheffield.
Although I like rugby,
I am a snooker fanatic.

Don't lecture me about lint on the baize –
I am ninety-six years of age.

I am frail and cranky
And I have a pain in my neck
That would make Humpty Dumpty
Grateful to fall of his wall,
But at a crucial moment in the Crucible
I sizzle with satisfaction
At the spectacle of a young man's bottom
As he bends down low over the green baize
To pot the black –

A superbly turned-out young man's trim bottom,
The left cheek of which is streamlined
With shoe heel and collar bone
When he lifts his left leg to spread-eagle it
Like a pedigree cocker spaniel
Along the kerb of the table.

Don't lecture me about lint on the baize –
I am ninety-six years of age.

And when that young man hails
From Ranelagh, Dublin 6,
And when his name is Ken
I am as much a believer in the Resurrection
As the Pope in Rome.
If there is a heaven –
One must not say so
But I doubt it –
Heaven would be the Triangle at night
Of snooker tables lit by floodlights
Under the whites of whose eyes
Thousands upon thousands
Of trim-bottomed young men
Would be chalking their cues
Before focussing their perfect pelvises

On the white cue ball,
The red and the black,
And on all the coloured balls –
All the coloured balls.

Don't lecture me about lint on the baize –
I am ninety-six years of age.

LOUIS MACNEICE

Soap Suds

This brand of soap has the same smell as once in the big
House he visited when he was eight: the walls of the
    bathroom open
To reveal a lawn where a great yellow ball rolls back
    through a hoop
To rest at the head of a mallet held in the hands of a child.

And these were the joys of that house: a tower with a
    telescope;
Two great faded globes, one of the earth, one of the stars;
A stuffed black dog in the hall; a walled garden with bees;
A rabbit warren; a rockery; a vine under glass; the sea.

To which he has now returned. The day of course is fine
And a grown-up voice cries Play! The mallet slowly
    swings,
Then crack, a great gong booms from the dog-dark hall
    and the ball
Skims forward through the hoop and then through the
    next and then

Through hoops where no hoops were and each dissolves
    in turn
And the grass has grown head-high and an angry voice
    cries Play!
But the ball is lost and the mallet slipped long since from
    the hands
Under the running tap that are not the hands of a child.

Darts & Shove Halfpenny

from 'Indoor Sports'

Darts

Begin and end with a double. He places his feet
Square apart on the rubber mat. I bet I shall end
As always on double one. The squeaking chalk
Subtracts, subtracts … What did I tell you? And why
Is it the hardest bed? Singles are useless
And there is no going back.

                            He flicks his wrist,
Hardly looking, and wins.

Shove halfpenny

On the field of elm or slate the lines are far too close;
The brass discs knock each other out of place.
You need a glancing blow with the ball of the thumb;
One disc can knock another one into place
With skill and join her there. No, not like that;
Like this.

              You see. Both safely between the lines.
With skill, as I said. And luck.

SEAMUS HEANEY

Squarings, III

Squarings? In the game of marbles, squarings
Were all those anglings, aimings, feints and squints
You were allowed before you'd shoot, all those

Hunkerings, tensings, pressures of the thumb,
Test-outs and pull-backs, re-envisagings,
All the ways your arms kept hoping towards

Blind certainties that were going to prevail
Beyond the one-off moment of the pitch.
A million million accuracies passed

Between your muscles' outreach and that space
Marked with three round holes and a drawn line.
You squinted out from a skylight of the world.

Marbles

Playing marbles in the avenue.
I loved their colours rolling on the path,
the spherical motion, the smack
when glass hit glass. We had fistfuls of them,
collections stashed in cloth bags
that we clutched like a treasure chest.
We exchanged and traded them.
Bluebottle blues for bloodshot reds.
It was part of the camaraderie of boys back then.
Kaleidoscopic, polished to the lustre of a gem,
sometimes they'd spill and fall,
pirouetting in all directions, slipping through
the grill and down the rain-shore.
A loss for which there was no consolation.

MATTHEW SWEENEY

The Glass Chess Set

He woke to find a glass chess set
by his head, on the bedside table.
The vitamins had been removed,
the lamp shifted to the floor,
the two glasses of water were gone –
all this done without a noise.
He sat up to see it better.
Everything was glass – the board,
the pieces, half of these clear,
half opaque, as were the alternating
squares. He got out of bed to
stand above it. One opaque pawn
had advanced, the clear team
nearest to him had made no move.
It was his turn. Who was
his invisible opponent? He opened
the shutters to let light in,
recalling his last game of chess
with his father. It had been Xmas.
He'd lost, of course, as always.
Well, he remembered winning once,
then refusing to play for years.
He glimpsed the set's reflection
in the mirror, saw for a second
a shadow stood there, then it was gone.
He sat down, studied the board,
and slowly, moved a clear pawn.

11
Boxing

DARAGH BREEN

Boxer

He has stepped, transfixed,
from the Gethsemane of
the ring, his forehead bearing
a crown of leaking,
ulcerous wounds

His arms hang
like Christ's limbs,
His own exhausted weight
having dragged Him
from the Cross

His knuckles, wrapped in
cheese cloth, are as pronounced
as the skeletal-ribcage
of a carved, crucified Christ,
still now, now still

PATRICK KAVANAGH

A Knight at the Tournament

Cole vs Mulcahy

It was not Virgil I thought of last Friday at the Rotunda
Or his verse which tells of huge muscled fighters
In the Roman arena as they exhibited their bodies to the
    nighters.
I was thinking of what I would say on Monday,
Something that all readers would understand – a
Hint of Tunney's lefts and Dempsey's righters
In the Soldiers Field … Cole swings, Mulcahy sidesteps.
The fight is on and the audience roars like thunder.
Blood flows. O Cole think back to Meath's great glory,
The battle fury of ancestors may descend
Upon you. But Mulcahy's footwork's perfect. Holy!
If that swing had got home the fight would end.
In the ninth round Mulcahy's science won,
Cole counted out. And here's your sonnet, Sir John.

The Boxers

We were combatants from the start. Our dad
Bought us boxing gloves when we were ten –
Champions like Euryalus, say, or Epeius
Of wooden-horse fame: 'I am the greatest!'
'Nobody's going to knock me down!' Listen,
Peter, to the commentary – gruesome teeth-
Grinding, sweat splattering their arms and legs,
Huge fists in ox-hide thongs slugging it out,
Then the knock-out blow to Euryalus's chin –
Hoisting him with an uppercut – like a fish
That arches out of weed-tangled shallows
And collapses back into hazy water,
Sea wind sending shock-waves up the beach –
The winner gives the loser a helping hand
And his seconds support him across the ring
On dragging feet, head lolling to one side,
Blood clots et cetera et cetera …
I'll tie your gloves. Shall we fight again?

DECLAN RYAN

Rope-a-Dope

Nothing for days, then a message:
'I want to see a fight. An old one,'
so I bring a fight to you.
You know nothing of these men;
even the most famous
get to slink in their youth again –
for you Foreman is Leviathan, unstoppable;
Ali just past his prime
flown 'home' to muscle back his title.
Not sure how you'll react to violence
we lie down again together –
your feet in woollen stockings
kneadable across my thighs,
your mouth close to my ribs
and their inmate: a pouting lifer.
I fidget and you scold.
As Ali opens up with right-hand leads
you flinch
but soon you're lost to the screen
where he waits it out along the ropes,
takes everything Foreman throws.
You don't believe he can soak up
all this pain and go on standing;
we cheer him on,
winter softened in the tropic of his strength.

When Ali comes alive to put Foreman on the ground
I see a hallelujah look as you turn to face me.
'He won,' you say into my cheek.
'He did,' I say.

12
Water Sports

EILÉAN NÍ CHUILLEANÁIN

The Last Glimpse of Erin

The coastline, a swimmer's polished shoulder heaving
On the edge of sky: our eyes make it grow:
The last glimpse, low and smooth in the sea.

We face the air, all surfaces become
Sheer, one long line is growing
Like a spider's navel cord: the distance

From your low shoulder lost in the quilt,
An arm thrown forward: a swimmer: your head
Buried in a pillow like a wave.

The white light skirting the cloud pierces
Glass riddled with small scratches and creates
The depths and cadences of a spider's web.

A man is holding his baby and laughing,
He strokes her cheek with a brownstained finger
While his wife sews a wristbutton on his other hand.

The island trimmed with waves is lost in the sea,
The swimmer lost in his dream.

SINÉAD MORRISSEY

Forty Lengths

Before goggles, the pool was a catch of beleaguered heads
being raced against each other by omnipotence.

But now that I, too, have been strapped back and capped
like a pre-war flying enthusiast –

shoulders to the rear, the aerodynamic necessity
of not having hair – I see

how solidly we occur under water.
Now all the world's a blur, except for down here

in this makeshift polar enclosure
where I follow one white-limbed swimmer after another

to the wall. We do not resemble fishes, so much as frogs
or the diving waterboatman with his fringed hind legs.

And I find myself back – to the womb,
most obviously, but even better than that – to the film

I played in my head as a child
to make myself sleep: me up in the sky

like Lucy, not needing to breathe, or be tired, or be told,
        or be older –
wishboning through the stratosphere.

PAT BORAN

Learning to Dive

The boy who is learning to dive
has a lot on his mind:

how to place
his unfamiliar, disobeying feet
on the slippery rungs;

how to straighten himself and walk
the length of the board
without glancing down;

how to stand, to extend
his arms straight ahead, as the other boys do,
without wavering;

how to cancel the height,
the shake in his legs,
once more how to breathe.

But while he stands there and the water stills,
from out of nowhere a kid half his size
goes charging past

to pedal pedal pedal in empty air,
before dropping through into the target
of his own reflection. Resounding cheers,

upon which the older boy gives up,
surrenders to something somewhere
beyond his control,

and at last steps clear
of the board to fall
away into the rapturous applause

of water, each glistening drop
a medal struck to honour his courage,
the triumph of his simply letting go.

LEONTIA FLYNN

Saturday in the Pool

The boy pauses at the end of the diving-board
then dives: a broad sword
cleaving the water – there is parting! And rejoining!
This is reflected back upon the ceiling
where, flippered, supine
– swimming in the cells
and water-pathways of ourselves –
we watch the gases breed: a fog of chlorine.

The boy pauses at the end of the diving-board
then dives: on board
the liberator, big-eyed airmen watch
as the cargo leaves the hatch:
the missile stabs the air
then impacts – megavolts
and gigawatts, primordial lightning bolts –
in whirlpool ripples: clouds of dust and vapour.

Saturday at the pool. A dozen forms
push. Kick. Breathe. Push. Kick. Breathe. Turn
and bring themselves along the tepid length
and breadth of the translucent element
like frogmen. Bone
and blood. Four dozen limbs
– nurses, teachers, wives, *civilians* –
push. Kick. Breathe. Push. Kick. Breathe. Turn.

Outside our youth is laid about the park.
Planes thread the sky like needles. No attack
presents itself. No dogfight
twists above the level of the trees. A kite
is moored in the sky. It peers,
like the boy on the diving-board, down upon the world
where we have crawled: we are raw-gilled
and live. The blood is banging in my ears.

Note: In the last line 'live' is the adjective, rhyming with 'five'.

CONOR O'CALLAGHAN

The End of the Line

is a pressure gauge touching red, running empty. Tap the Enter key and – there! –
a solidus of light is thrown across your path from the balcony above.
It helps to think of some fat lute shod in espadrilles. It helps to sing of love,
between each blip whereby your song excuses itself to the cool night air.
It should get to feel like those seconds following sex, their little death
made littler still by missed beats just like that and the fear that all oxygen is gone
halfway down the next and you're bound for that plot the muses call 'Anon'.
You're not. Relax. Thank your lucky stars they're full of stops to catch your breath.

This is how I learned. In shallows cordoned off for paddling and kids, I found
it took the baker's dozen sideways sucks to tip the far wall and come back
it takes to say a sonnet whole. I climb a lane, balloon my lungs to the diaphragm
(where did the balcony go? where did you? where has this pool arrived from?)
and fall too hard for that point of no return where the water looms deep and black.
This is when it comes: drained of noise, night without rungs, no lifeguards around.

Swimming Out

– for M.C.

We spent most of that Summer
under the watchful gaze of the lifeguard.
However, the glowing orange buoy
marking the lobster pots,
easily discernible about a mile out,
haunted our every dreary, shore-hugging swim.
One morning we set out to reach it,
whatever the consequences.
Your brothers joined us
for the first quarter of a mile,
then turned back, warning of dire perils.
We swam on steadily,
two tanned striplings cutting through
the sparkle and glitter
of the early morning ocean,
the tightening silence broken
by the plash plash of our measured strokes
and the flick and ripple
from our trailing feet.
A shoal of sprat brushed past us
at full-pelt and finally unleashed
our pent-up terrors, resulting in
a mad sprint over the last hundred yards to the buoy.
We reached it,
amazed and a little daunted,

by the distance we had covered
and the blue shimmering depths beneath us.
We could just make out the tiny figures
of your brothers running up and down the beach,
waving frantically.
Tired but elated, we began
the long swim home.

MARY O'MALLEY

Surfing

– for Oisín

Yesterday at seven o'clock a triangle of sky
between the asphalt, the Marine Science Building
and lush July trees took wing. It filled with the din
of young swallows, twittering weapons

flung on the increased air, making space liquid.
They scissor out of nowhere, junior jet pilots
not crashing once. This is a slice of day cut by Magritte.
The cubists deny there is a vanishing point.

This expanding envelope supports them.
The clean sky is threatened. Nearby a tree
planted in memory of a boy calls this wonder fragile.
Who was he? I think of his brief grace, his early fall.

At last you phone. Gone surfing with your friends,
black and swooping as those swallows
skating the glass slope of a wave
between dark and dark in this diamond of time.

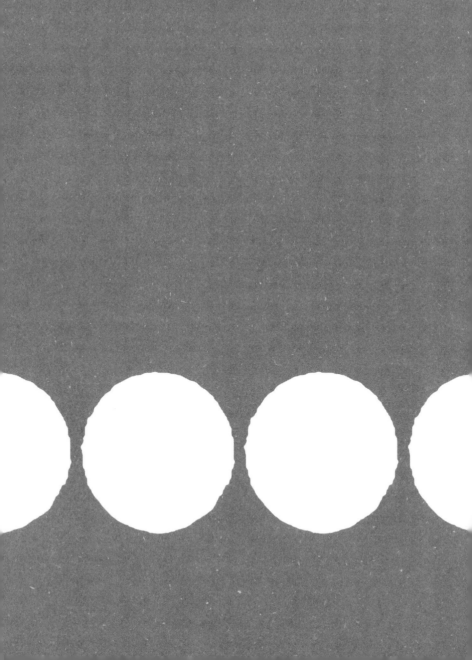

13

Hurling & Camogie

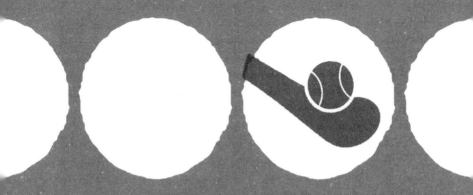

PAUL DURCAN

The One-Armed Crucifixion

– after Giacomo Manzù

How many thousands of hours on the shore at Galway,
In the drizzle off the back of the sea,
On the sodden sands,
Did we spend hurling together, father and son?
Pucking the *sliotar*, one to the other,
Hour in, hour out, year in, year out.
How many thousands of times, old man,
Did you strike a high ball for your young son
To crouch, to dart, to leap,
To pluck the ball one-handed out of the climbing air?

Camogie

Gaelic Sunday at New Eltham,
a match from home over the radio,
awkward, incongruous colours
on the women, children delving
into imported packets of Oatfield sweets.

Back in the city of the Tribes,
the blonde girl practising camogie.
Bending, lifting, striking effortlessly.
At Nimmo's pier, Jenny
watching piebald horses
and imaginary Arab stallions.

The flags down for the game,
the *sliotar* in the air,
her face among the others,
healthy girls in their prime,
players all out of position
following a thing in flight.

PATRICK KAVANAGH

Camogie Match

Bright shone the sunlight on Peggy and Doreen,
Wild swung the ash sticks. Be careful astooreen;
Josie is getting right into her stride now,
Kathleen is hurling with all her Cork pride now.
A shout from the side-line: 'Mark your man,
     Kathleen Cody.'
Kathleen pucks it. I tell you that puck was a dotie.
The game is exciting, it is indeed really,
Maureen Cashman is tackling bold Ide O'Kiely …

JOHN FITZGERALD

Ecstasis

If there is
to have been one
moment, it could be this:
body sprung from turf, suspended,
ash-stick hoisted, level and at bay,
arm aloft to pluck a rough-seamed purse
of rag and yarn and glory from the sky;
that instant, all elements of body
and mind outstrained to reach for
the impossible, when, into my
hand like a bird
it came.

LIAM MURPHY

Donal Foley Played Hurling with my Father

my fathers funeral stops outside theatre royal
beside corporation yard where he worked and died
near where we lived and laughed in my childhood
closeby on the river his boat floats
on a flood of memories

mourners from behind the hearse
shake my shaken hand and commiserate
  pat fanning from the gaa
    my youth was measured
    in hurley sizes
  joe cummins from fianna fáil
    who kept his promise
    and helped with medical card
  knox brennan labour mayor
    who knew poems
    and promised a book on byron
and the man who said
donal foley played hurling
with your father god rest him

my fathers funeral stops
people gather
and I can't stop it happening

I am alone in new white shirt
and new black tie
in the suit I got married in
my father dies in his overalls
and I can't stop it happening

a doctor takes me aside
too shocked for tears
no last messages
no sad goodbyes

there is a bandage
on his finger in the coffin
my wife carries the grandson
he will never see
my fathers funeral stops
a rosary begins

buy drink for family and friends
sedative for mother
same man still telling me
donal foley played hurling
with my father

the funeral stops.

BRYAN MACMAHON

A Song for Christy Ring

to the air of 'Old Skibbereen'

Come gather round me boys to-night and raise your glasses high;
Come Rockies, 'Barrs and Rover stars, let welcome hit the sky,
Let bonfires blaze in heroes praise, Let Shannon echoes fling,
For homeward bound with hurling crown comes gallant
    Christy Ring.

To every man his game and sport, as every man his creed;
But where's the race that can compare with Cork's own
    hurling breed,
As fair and free in fierce melee that ash and leather sling,
And swift among the blades outflung moves peerless
    Christy Ring?

So all you hurlers from the Nore, you lads from Corrib's side,
From Garryowen gay and bold, with Tipp's own men beside,
You may have hurlers straight and brave who can a *camán* swing,
But whose the name can play the game with Cork's own
    Christy Ring?

When we were young we read at school that in the days of old,
The young Setanta showed his worth with shield and spear
    of gold,
As hurling hard on Royal sward he'd Red Branch heroes fling,
My soul to-day, he'd yield the sway if he met Christy Ring.

A health to faithful Wexford, boys, to the Rackards and
        their team,
Should Cork surrender Ireland's Crown may victory on
        them gleam,
John Kelly's name we hold in fame – of '98 we sing,
But Slaney's plan must find a man to equal Christy Ring.

How oft I've watched him from the hill move here and there
        in grace,
In Cork, Killarney, Thurles Town or by the Shannon's Race,
'Now Cork is be't, the hay is saved!' the thousands wildly sing –
They speak too soon, my sweet gorsoon, for here comes
        Christy Ring!

When age has gained this warrior brave, when ended is
        the fight,
And o'er the hearth he hangs at last his stick and trophies bright,
Come Counties all both great and small who boast a
        hurling King,
Can one to-night hold candlelight to Cork's own Christy Ring?

THEO DORGAN

Learning My Father's Memories

I saw Cúchulainn in his latter years,
great knots of muscle in his shoulders,
the gleaming dome of his skull in the afternoon.

I saw him drive younger warriors from the field
by the fierce power of his eye on the frozen ball,
his gift for gathering and unleashing force.

He fought each autumn match through a fog of glories
already legend, the air he prowled in doubled,
and his step doubled with a younger self.

I saw his last matches for The Glen, the young bucks
already impatient to sweep him to the heavens
where blood and raw knuckles, mud and defeat

or victory would fade into remembered youth –
a child myself, I sensed their insensate cruelty,
the watchful precise impatience of the young.

Powerful because legend, his powers already fading,
each match by then a match with himself only,
the grammar of ageing played out in the Mardyke mud.

Christ, he was younger then than I am now!
My father's age, who seemed so old to me then,
and now so young. So it goes on, the old parade

through sweat and mud and memory, the hero,
his followers and his fellow warriors …
And back there on the grass-banked terrace

a round-eyed child in his own fog of doubt,
testing the fix in a spin of words and meanings:
'That's him, I'm looking at him, Christy Ring.'

BILLY RAMSELL

Lament for Christy Ring

– to my father

after Seán Ó Tuama

Aboriginal, electrical,
his great bulging eye

amid the stadium's temper,
amid the furies and exultations
of the great-coated stands,
as he lopes in a bull's diagonal goal-ward.

Improbable balance
of ball on broad *bas*,
on his stick of ashy liquidity
that's rippling, eel-flexible, alive.

And now his body it is liquid too,
an impressionist version of itself
as he slights the wall of three defenders,
pours himself through some improbable gap
and on the other side re-solidifies.

He swerves, ducks his shoulder, elegantly jerks.
And what gap now between thought and act,
his spirit and firmware fusing?

And is it only in his own mind
the underwater silence for his backswing,
for his shape's familiar coil into potential,
for the glance, the pull and the connection?

And the cork-hearted ball
becomes nothing at all,
is too nimble, too cute for the eye
and the goalkeeper's beaten,
and Clare and Tipp and Kilkenny are beaten
and the terraces inhale themselves
and the air is vibrating in shock and in awe.

Patricia Horgan's would be the last face he saw.
She would step out for the messages
and walk into history.
She would go to buy butter
and become a minor character.

His chest clenched, clenched and accelerated,
bucked and ratcheted,
in the eye of the forming throng
as he flopped there watching
behind her cow-eyed gentle expression
the usual mergers of cumulus, a crow,

and the gulls at their shrill affairs over Morrison's Island
until the clouds themselves clouded over.

She said: *Ní fheádfaí an fear sin a adhlacadh.*
Mór an peaca an fear sin a adhlacadh.
You couldn't bury that man.
It'd be a sin to bury that man.

And to this day I still can't bury Christy Ring.

We'll carry his washed and scented remains,
in procession, by candlelight, by hand-held electric light,
from the cemetery at Cloyne
to an undisclosed location in the midlands,

shoulder him into a mossed-over dome,
to the burial room
through the long corbelled tunnel,
and in that chamber of must and slow-tutting stones
lay him out on a bier of amethyst
that's been carved, that's been perfumed
with palm and with cinnamon.
And on all sides
the surprisingly petite skeletons of our ancestors,
the priests, the chieftains,
all the princes of swordplay and laughter:

their careful lines of dowry and cousinship
all merged in a carpet of loam,
the victories, the enmities rusted,
and the quarrels, ah the quarrels all gone,
the quarrels all long processed by worms.

Leave him there in that society of bone
and walk back through sock-drenching grasses,
the spiders and the daisies, water cresses,
past one particular field of rape outside Edgeworthstown
that stretches in primrose,
that soaks up the buttery sunlight of late morning,
that never knew his name to forget it.

ENDA WYLEY

On My Father's Birthday

I saw silvery ancient lichen
that grows where the air is pure,

deep tap roots of the marram grass
holding the sand-dunes up –

those grasses we painted as children,
stood in jam-jars on our windowsills –

a cargo boat crossing the bay,

a dead sea-gull
his legs frozen and green,

the dog whelk shell I blew sand from
and later balanced on the bath edge,

the fluorescent pink dome of the Italian circus tent
far across in Booterstown, its lions roaring like sea,

sky-larks singing spring in,

sand under our nails and grating
the backs of our throats like arguments,

brent geese on mud-flats feeding on eel-grass
far from a Greenland peninsula,

bladderwrack sticking to stone
with a glue scientists crave,

ringed plovers and sanderlings,

oyster catchers with their twitting sounds
more high-pitched than the nervous gulls,

car windows glinting on James Larkin Memorial Road,
his hands a constant memory raised up over O'Connell
      Street,

terns flying away from Kilbarrack flats
and a top-shell shaped like an emperor's hat,

St Mary Star of the Sea, a holy stilt walker,

on the beach the red-coated father carrying one child
on his shoulder, laughing at the others racing the tide,

behind them a Sunday car sinking in the sand,
moss crawling up Mary's hundred-feet-high stone legs.

And they are us and you long before this day,
Calling the sea a name we'd never heard before –

Thalassa, Thalassa, Thalassa,

and we chase after the *sliotar*
your hurley gives to those holiday waves,

we are young pups walking home with you over rabbits
sleeping deep in the sandy dunes of Cruit Island,

we are waiting for fresh fish got
from the currachs at Carrickfinn,

we are waiting for stories to come.

TOM FRENCH

A Laminated Hurley

from 'Late Encounters'

His hurley fallen asunder in his hands,
I come upon him, like the child in the tale
on a mission, bearing the thing that will change
everything if he can arrive in time

and thwart fate, gathering *cippins* on his hands
and knees in the six yard box of the pitch
they took the hill from, and I am tempted
to kneel and help him.

Because it had no grain it had no spring,
and there was no one tree its timber came from.
To *French* through *de Freyne* from *Fraxinus*,
my father's name comes down to me from *ash*.

14
American Sports

FRANK MCGUINNESS

American Football
in Booterstown Park

After six months the grass grows again.
The Christmas ice rink very few wanted –
that's long dismantled and melted in rain.
Nobody weeps for its loss – we're well rid
of figures of eight the skaters circled,
taking deep breaths as if life depended
on staying erect. The freezing fires of hell
wait for those damned by what's been done and said.
Time to bury all that is bitter and dark:
the summer's come back to Booterstown Park.

Their fat loins girded, their elegant arse
bound tight as most delicate Chinese feet,
sharp to the touch like the yellowest gorse,
American footballers congregate.
They do not entirely understand the score
of the game they play against each other
engaging in what is uncivil war –
brother beating the crap out of brother.
They live for the logo they choose to wear.
Blood is thicker than mineral water.

June brings these migratory birds to us,
searching for diamonds in the Bird Sanctuary.
A sign of intelligent life, a cause –
just to believe in the land of the free.
I wait an age for the Number 7,

rattling the fare in my jeans pocket.
I could throw money – pennies from heaven –
to bless the boys in their ludicrous kit.
They have eyes only for the task in hand.
To win, to touch down – that I understand.

I hear the medley of each dialect
from the four corners of this island
at the Sunday game, risking their neck
to score for the parish across the ocean.
More power to their arm, their fist, the caul
at the top of their most breakable scalp –
they watch the birdie, they rise and they fall,
they give the bastards opposite a skelp.
They pray for rain to drench the playing fields:
they look to the earth for a better yield.

They have the luck to be clean as whistles,
and nothing is stained by the blood of slaves.
Let us salute them as knights of the realm,
domain of the paleskin, home of the brave.
Their holdalls contain the robes of saffron,
Argyll socks, winklepickers, kipper ties –
strange uniforms of a lost dimension
where nobody ever has to say goodbye.
The sea disgorged these dolphins and sharks:
American Football in Booterstown Park.

CONOR O'CALLAGHAN

Game Night

Love not
being in the loop.

Grant the spruces' wish,
the golf compound
greying out of use,
SUVs in the IT lot,
power outage,
a chorus from the quad.

Bless the elsewhere
where others are
not here or you.

And rain
after midnight ...
Ask yourself,
is that rain or bells?

GREG DELANTY

Tagging the Stealer

– to David Cavanagh

So much of it I hadn't a bull's notion of
and like the usual ignoramus who casts his eyes
at, say, a Jackson Pollock or 'This Is Just to Say',
I scoffed at it. I didn't twig how it was as close
to art as art itself with its pre-game ballyhoo,
antics, rhubarbs, scheming, luck; its look
as if little or nothing is going on.
How often have we waited for the magic
in the hands of some flipper throwing a slider,
sinker, jug-handle, submarine, knuckle or screwball?
If we're lucky, the slugger hits a daisy cutter
with a choke-up or connects with a Baltimore chop
and a ball hawk catches a can of corn
with a basket catch and the ball rounds the horn.
Oh, look, Davo, how I'm sent sailing
right out of the ball park just by its lingo.
But I swear the most memorable play I witnessed
was with you on our highstools in the Daily Planet
as we slugged our Saturday night elixirs.
The Yankees were playing your Toronto Blue Jays.
They were tied at the top of the 9th.
I can't now for the life of me remember
who won, nor the name of the catcher, except
he was an unknown, yet no rookie.
Suddenly behind the pinch hitter's back he signalled

the pitcher, though no one copped until seconds later
as the catcher fireballed the potato to the first baseman,
tagging the stealer. It doesn't sound like much,
but everyone stood up round the house Ruth built
like hairs on the back of the neck, because the magic
was scary too. Jesus, give each of us just once
a poem the equal of that unknown man's talking hand.

PAUL MULDOON

Chunkey

A game about which we've got next to nothing straight,
it seems to have been a mash-up of *buzkashi* and road bowls.
As I try to anticipate a spear-thrower trying to anticipate
the spot where the chunkey-stone rolls

to a standstill, I hear a ten thousand strong shout
go up over the abandoned chunkey-yard at Cahokia,
    in support,
maybe, of the idea Cahokia will win out.
Maybe we should accept our understanding must fall short

as a spear falls short of this sandstone disk
some take to represent the sun.
Maybe we should accept our grand ambitions as grandiose

and our aversion to averting risk
merely rash. Maybe we should support the idea that
    having won
will mean merely 'to have come close'.

15
Rugby & Cricket

Rugby Football Excursion

Euston – the smell of soot and fish and petrol;
Then in the train jogging and jogging,
The sheaf of wires from pole to pole beside us
Dogging the fancy northward

And waking to board the *Hibernia* – Bass and Guinness,
Bull-necks and brogues and favours
And Kerry-coloured girls; the whole excursion
Savours of twelve years back

Back to my adolescence, back to Ireland
"Ilkla Moor ba't a't" from Midland voices,
And Wicklow apricot in early sunshine
Rejoices what was jaded.

Horse-cabs and outside cars – the ballyhoo for trippers –
And College Park reposeful behind the railings;
Emphatic old ladies' voices in a lounge lamenting
Failings of health and budgets.

Lansdowne Road – the swirl of faces, flags,
Gilbert and Sullivan music, emerald jerseys;
Spire and crane beyond remind the mind on furlough
Of Mersey's code and Rome's.

Eccentric scoring – Nicholson, Marshall and Unwin,
Replies by Bailey and Daly;
Rugs around our shins, the effortless place-kick
Gaily carving the goalposts.

Then tea and toast with Fellows and Bishops in a huge
Regency room in the warmth of a classic assurance
Looking on Stephen's Green where they blew up George
    the Second –
Endurance of one-way thinking.

And then a walk through Dublin down the great
Grey streets broad and straight and drowned in twilight,
Statues of poets and Anglo-Irish patriots –
High lights of merged traditions.

Junkshops, the smell of poverty, pubs at the corner,
A chimney on fire and street on street of broken
Fanlights over the doors of tenement houses –
Token of the days of Reason.

In a frame from Sir Isaac Newton the dusk of Ireland
Bathes the children whipping their tops on the cobbles
Or swinging by ropes from a lamp post while a cripple
Hobbles like a Hogarth sketch.

These I must leave, rejoin the beery trippers
Whose other days prefer today delirious
Packing the bar on the boat, while a sapphire pinhead
Sirius marks Dún Laoghaire.

JOHN O'DONNELL

Team Photo

One joker up on tiptoe at the back;
centre, the proud captain, holding ball. Arms
folded in a swagger, we were ready

for anything the world could hurl at us.
Pirate beards, teen-idol hair – the glamour:
we were sure to knock 'em dead

in the bar after. Boots crusting with pitch-muck
and tradition; the jerseys that on fired-up afternoons
we'd sworn we'd die for. And (not in picture)

the all-in-this-together of it, lingering here
like the reek of Deep Heat in the changing-room
as players take the field to scattered cheers.

THOMAS MCCARTHY

The Cappoquin Cricket XI

Memory is a *plein air* studio,
contemporaneous, ourselves looking on:
like this Edwardian afternoon in Cappoquin.
It is a resolute moment above our town,
a game of cricket ended. Eleven men
kneel down awhile before letting go.

Young men, no doubt, from the best families
                     of my native town,
the top eleven of the freehold name-plates.
Each one is at ease with the photographer
twelve years before the Free State
made such self-assurance legitimate:

Frahers, Oldens and Whites, Collenders
and Walshes, a young Kenny from the square,
Laceys born to be factory managers,
Barrons and Currans, Bolgers and Sargents.
Boarding-schools and monsignor uncles
will uplift the more banal trades.

Here we find the past at its most naked,
men fully dressed in cricket whites, prosperous,
not an Ireland to be imagined or made
whole in national speeches, but the thing itself:

social power and its immortal oneness
as well-connected as a Diocesan priest.

One player with flowing black curls
and perfect smiling teeth, he'll inherit
an import business and a river boat.
A youth with eyes and mouth that never smile
will make his fortune as a Sweepstake agent.
None of them, as far as I can tell,
will lose in love; none will marry a local.

Connections will be made from other towns.
Middle-class in a poor, congested land,
their destinies seem relentless, destined.
A nation awake, soviets and flying columns,
to the very end nothing disturbs the pattern.
Bourgeois chances were theirs to take

on afternoons never as tendentious
as my own bitter speculation is.
Words are things I hurl from Twig Bog Lane.
They stick for a moment to such perfect ease:
a simple photograph, the white comfort
of sport. Only, my childhood is a jealous critic
and burns the plate at their bended knees.

GERARD FANNING

Offering the Light

If three white on the score board
should lead to an offer
to abandon the day's endeavour,
I'll play the night watchman

who heads for the pavilion
taking for company
a last glance round silly point,
a brief sweep of boundary and bye

and one more entry
for that loose archive,
where the real map of Dublin
is about the same size as Dublin.

16
The Dogs

PAUL MULDOON

At Master McGrath's Grave

I.

He had a long white streak
On his deep chest,
A small white patch
Over one of his shoulders,
And two white claws
On each of his forepaws.

Over his lean back
He was all ticked with white,
As if a shower of hail
Had fallen and never melted.

II.

Should he not still smoulder,
Our shooting star,
That claimed the Waterloo Cup
In eighteen sixty-nine?

I'm standing at the edge
Of Lord Lurgan's demesne
Where the Master is stretched

Under his plinth,
A bucket of quicklime
Scattered all along his length.

III.

The overhanging elm-trees
And the knee-high grass
Are freshly tinged
By this last sun-shower.
I'm not beside myself with grief,
Not even so taken by McGrath,

It's just the way these elm-trees
Do more and more impinge,
The knee-high grass
Has brought me to my knees.

CIARAN CARSON

Night Music

In the burned-down library
a man manipulates a keyboard
searching for a passage in the cloud
that might shed light
on what he has in mind
the constellations glitter overhead
in roofless space
from time to time
the wind kicks a tin can down the street
a roulette trickle
stops and starts
shouts from the crowd
in a floodlit stadium
greyhounds pursue the grey electric being
that eludes them time
and time again.

MAURICE RIORDAN

The Holy Land

Father Burns has given us Basil, his greyhound pup,
while he's away himself to the Holy Land.
Basil's track name is Goldfinger.
We believe he's the fastest hound in Christendom.

When he runs round the house his nose appears
at one gable before his tail is gone at the other,
but when we take him to Buttevant for trial
he freezes at the sound of the electric hare.

Although she's loth to vilify a beast
on whom the priest has pinned his hopes,
I hear my mother say under her breath
The little bastard, when he roots up the lily bed.

Basil still streaks around the house
now Father Burns is home and has projected
the holy sights onto Smarts' loft wall: mosaics
and basilicas; Gethsemane, the Mount of Olives.

Then the minibus north through Judea
and Galilee – to Capernaum, Cana,
the water on which He walked, Nazareth
where He was a boy. There too is a basilica.

ACKNOWLEDGEMENTS

'A Spin in the Rain with Seamus Heaney' by PAUL DURCAN from *Life is a Dream: 40 Years Reading Poems 1967-2007* (Harvill Secker, 2009), by kind permission of the author and Rogers, Coleridge and White, 20 Powis Mews, London, W11 1JN. 'The Game of Tennis in Irish History' by VONA GROARKE from *Juniper Street* (2006), by kind permission of the author and The Gallery Press, Loughcrew, Oldcastle, Co Meath. 'The Difference' by IGGY MCGOVERN from *The King of Suburbia* (2006), by kind permission of the author and Dedalus Press, 13 Moyclare Rd, Baldoyle, Dublin 13. 'Tennis in Wicklow' by FERGUS ALLEN from *Mrs Power Looks Over the Bay* (1999), by kind permission of the author and Faber and Faber, Bloomsbury House, 74-77 Great Russell St, London. 'How to Play Championship Tennis' by PAUL MULDOON from *Mules* (1977), by kind permission of the author and Faber and Faber, Bloomsbury House, 74-77 Great Russell St, London. 'Footballer' by PÁDRAIG J. DALY from *The Voice of the Hare* (1997), by kind permission of the author and Dedalus Press, 13 Moyclare Rd, Baldoyle, Dublin 13. 'Station Island, VII' by SEAMUS HEANEY from *Station Island* (1984), by kind permission of the author's estate and Faber and Faber, Bloomsbury House, 74-77 Great Russell St, London. 'Munster Football Final 1924' by GABRIEL FITZMAURICE from *The Lonesome Road: Collected and New Poems 1984-2014* (2014), by kind permission of the author and Liberties Press, 140 Terenure Rd North, Dublin. 'Munster Final' by BERNARD O'DONOGHUE from *The Weakness* (Chatto and Windus, 1991), by kind permission of the author. 'The Football Field' by NOEL MONAHAN from *Where the Wind Sleeps* (2014), by kind permission of the author and Salmon Poetry, Knockeven, Cliffs of Moher, Co Clare. 'The Point' by SEAMUS HEANEY from *Seeing Things* (1991), by kind permission of the author's estate and Faber and Faber, 74-77 Great Russell St, London. 'Minding Goal' by PATRICK DEELEY from *Turane: The Hidden Village* (1995), by kind permission of the author and Dedalus Press, 13 Moyclare Rd, Baldoyle, Dublin 13. 'Reconstructionists' by MICHAEL HARTNETT from *A Book of Strays* (2002), by kind permission of the author's estate and The Gallery Press, Loughcrew, Oldcastle, Co Meath. 'The Madness of Football' by BRENDAN KENNELLY from *The Book of Judas* (1992), by kind permission of the author and Bloodaxe Books, Eastburn, South Park, Hexham, Northumberland. 'A Religious Occasion' by BRENDAN KENNELLY from *The Book of Judas* (1991), by kind permission of the author and Bloodaxe Books, Eastburn, South Park, Hexham, Northumberland. 'Hay' by PETER FALLON from *The News and Weather* (1987), by kind permission of the author and The Gallery Press, Loughcrew, Oldcastle, Co Meath. 'Croke Park or Ballylee, 1989' by BERNARD O'DONOGHUE from *The Weakness* (Chatto and Windus, 1991), by kind permission of the author. 'A Man's World' by MARTINA EVANS from *Facing the Public* (2009), by kind permission of the author and Anvil Press, Neptune House, 70 Royal Hill Rd, London. 'Sport' by PAUL DURCAN from *Life is a Dream: 40 Years Reading Poems 1967-2007* (Harvill Secker, 2009), by kind permission of the author and Rogers, Coleridge and White, 20 Powis Mews, London, W11 1JN. 'The Three Card Trick Man' by PEGGIE GALLAGHER from *Tilth* (2013), by kind permission of the author and Arlen House, PO Box 222, Galway. 'The Race Field' by TOM FRENCH from *The Fire Step* (2009), by kind permission of the author and The Gallery Press, Loughcrew, Oldcastle, Co Meath. 'Laytown Races, 1959' by GERARD FANNING from *Hombre: New and Selected Poems* (2011), by kind permission of the author and Dedalus Press, 13 Moyclare Rd, Baldoyle, Dublin 13. 'Gowran Park, Autumn Meeting' by PADRAIC FALLON from *Collected Poems* (1990), by kind permission of the author's estate and The Gallery Press, Loughcrew, Oldcastle, Co Meath. 'At Galway Races' by W.B. YEATS from *Complete Poems* (1990), published by J.M. Dent, Orion Publishing Group, Orion House, 5 Upper St Martin's Lane, London. 'The Racing Festival' by TOM DUDDY from *The Hiding Place* (2011), by kind permission of the author's estate and Arlen House, PO Box 222, Galway. 'Action Replays' by FRANK ORMSBY from *The Ghost Train* (1995), by kind permission of the author and The Gallery Press, Loughcrew, Oldcastle, Co Meath. 'Lone Patrol' by MARY NOONAN from *The Fado House* (2012), by kind permission of the author and Dedalus Press, 13 Moyclare Rd, Baldoyle, Dublin 13. 'The Old Jockey' by F.R. HIGGINS from *Father and Son: Selected Poems* (2014), by kind permission of the author and Arlen House, PO Box 222, Galway. 'The Wide World' by MARTINA EVANS from *All Alcoholics Are Charmers* (1998), by kind permission of the author and Anvil Press, Neptune House, 70 Royal Hill Rd, London. 'The Yellow Golf Ball on the Lawn' by MATTHEW SWEENEY from *Horse Music* (2013), by kind permission of the author and Bloodaxe Books, Eastburn, South Park, Hexham, Northumberland. 'He Begins with a Line by Sandy Lyle' by MAURICE RIORDAN from *The Holy Land* (2007), by kind permission of the author and Faber and Faber, Bloomsbury House, 74-77 Great Russell St, London. 'Pitch & Putt' by CONOR O'CALLAGHAN from *Seatown* (1999), by kind permission of the author and The Gallery Press, Loughcrew, Oldcastle, Co Meath. 'Moonshine' by DAVID WHEATLEY from *Misery Hill* (2000), by kind permission of the author and The Gallery Press, Loughcrew, Oldcastle, Co Meath. 'Poetry' by JOHN O'DONNELL from *On Water* (2014), by kind permission of the author and Dedalus Press, 13 Moyclare Rd, Baldoyle, Dublin 13. 'Remembering Certain Golf Holes' by DERMOT BOLGER from *That Which Is Suddenly Precious: New and Selected Poems* (2015), by kind permission of the author and New Island Books, 16 Priory Hall Office Park, Stillorgan, Co Dublin. 'Squarings, XI' by SEAMUS HEANEY from *Seeing Things* (1991), by kind permission of the author's estate and Faber and Faber, Bloomsbury House, 74-77 Great Russell St, London. 'Handball Legend' by MARTIN DYAR from *Maiden Names* (2013), by kind permission of the author and Arlen House, PO Box 222, Galway. 'After Viewing *The Bowling Match at Castlemary, Cloyne, 1847*' by GREG DELANTY from *Collected Poems 1986-2006* (2006), by kind permission of the author and Carcanet Press, Alliance House, 30 Cross St, Manchester. 'Manager, Perhaps' by BRENDAN KENNELLY from *The Essential Brendan Kennelly: Selected Poems* (2011), by kind permission of the author and Bloodaxe Books, Eastburn, South Park, Hexham, Northumberland. 'Goals' by ROBERT GREACEN from *Selected and New Poems* (2006), by kind permission of the author's estate and Salmon Poetry, Knockeven, Cliffs of Moher, Co Clare.

ACKNOWLEDGEMENTS

'George Best' by DAVID PARK, by kind permission of the author. 'Tinkerness' by MIRIAM GAMBLE from *The Squirrels are Dead* (2010), by kind permission of the author and Bloodaxe Books, Eastburn, South Park, Hexham, Northumberland. 'Ryan Giggs is a Ride' by ELAINE FEENEY from *The Radio Was Gospel* (2013), by kind permission of the author and Salmon Poetry, Knockeven, Cliffs of Moher, Co Clare. 'The Beautiful Game' by PAUL DURCAN from *Life is a Dream: 40 Years Reading Poems 1967-2007* (Harvill Secker, 2009), by kind permission of the author and Rogers, Coleridge and White, 20 Powis Mews, London, W11 1JN. 'If There Was Time All Day to Wait' by ALAN GILLIS from *Here Comes the Night* (2010), by kind permission of the author and The Gallery Press, Loughcrew, Oldcastle, Co Meath. 'Ireland Is Changing Mother' by RITA ANN HIGGINS from *Ireland Is Changing Mother* (2011), by kind permission of the author and Bloodaxe Books, Eastburn, South Park, Hexham, Northumberland. 'Soccer Moms' by PAUL MULDOON from *Horse Latitudes* (2006), by kind permission of the author and Faber and Faber, Bloomsbury House, 74-77 Great Russell St, London. 'The Fathers Raising The Nets for the Last Game of the Season: A Triptych' by TOM FRENCH from *Cyphers 79* (Spring/Summer 2015), by kind permission of the author and *Cyphers*, 3 Selskar Terrace, Ranelagh, Dublin 6. 'Sports Day' by JOHN O'DONNELL from *Some Other Country* (2002), by kind permission of the author and Bradshaw Books, Thompson House, MacCurtain St, Cork. 'Running with the Immortals' by THEO DORGAN from *Greek* (2010), by kind permission of the author and Dedalus Press, 13 Moyclare Rd, Baldoyle, Dublin 13. 'Great North' by COLETTE BRYCE from the *Guardian* (10/07/2010), by kind permission of the author. 'Keeping in Shape' by GERRY MURPHY from *End of Part One: New and Selected Poems* (2006), by kind permission of the author and Dedalus Press, 13 Moyclare Rd, Baldoyle, Dublin 13. 'Bicycle' by VINCENT WOODS from *Poetry Ireland Review 107* (2012), by kind permission of the author. 'The Cyclist' by LOUIS MACNEICE from *Collected Poems* (2007), by kind permission of the author's estate and Faber and Faber, Bloomsbury House, 74-77 Great Russell St, London. 'Bikes' by JOHN F. DEANE from *Snow Falling on Chestnut Hill: New and Selected Poems* (2012), by kind permission of the author and Carcanet Press, Alliance House, 30 Cross St, Manchester. 'Two Brothers Up' by SEBASTIAN BARRY from *The Water-Colourist* (1983), by kind permission of the author and Derek Johns / United Agents, 12-26 Lexington Street, London. 'Fisherman' by PATRICK DEELEY from *Groundswell: New and Selected Poems* (2013), by kind permission of the author and Dedalus Press, 13 Moyclare Rd, Baldoyle, Dublin 13. 'Finding the Ox' by CIARAN CARSON from *The Twelfth of Never* (1999), by kind permission of the author and The Gallery Press, Loughcrew, Oldcatle, Co Meath. 'The Curée' by CAITRÍONA O'REILLY from *The Sea Cabinet* (2006), by kind permission of the author and Bloodaxe Books, Eastburn, South Park, Hexham, Northumberland. 'Seeing Things' by PAULA CUNNINGHAM from *Heimlich's Manoeuvre* (2013), by kind permission of the author and Smith|Doorstop Books, Bank St Arts, 32-40 Bank St, Sheffield, UK. 'Green Baize Couplets' by CONOR O'CALLAGHAN from *Seatown* (1999), by kind permission of the author and The Gallery Press, Loughcrew, Oldcastle, Co

Meath. 'The 2003 World Snooker Championship' by PAUL DURCAN from *Life is a Dream: 40 Years Reading Poems 1967-2007* (Harvill Secker, 2009), by kind permission of the author and Rogers, Coleridge and White, 20 Powis Mews, London, W11 1JN. 'Soap Suds' by LOUIS MACNEICE from *Collected Poems* (2007), by kind permission of the author's estate and Faber and Faber, Bloomsbury House, 74-77 Great Russell St, London. 'Darts' and 'Shove halfpenny' by LOUIS MACNEICE from *Collected Poems* (2007), by kind permission of the author's estate and Faber and Faber, Bloomsbury House, 74-77 Great Russell St, London. 'Squarings, III' by SEAMUS HEANEY from *Seeing Things* (1991), by kind permission of the author's estate and Faber and Faber, Bloomsbury House, 74-77 Great Russell St, London. 'Marbles' by GERARD SMYTH from *The Fullness of Time: New and Selected Poems* (2010), by kind permission of the author and Dedalus Press, 13 Moyclare Rd, Baldoyle, Dublin 13. 'The Glass Chess Set' by MATTHEW SWEENEY from *Horse Music* (2013), by kind permission of the author and Bloodaxe Books, Eastburn, South Park, Hexham, Northumberland. 'Boxer' by DARAGH BREEN from *Whale* (2010), by kind permission of the author and November Press, Kilmacabea, Leap, Co Cork. 'A Knight at the Tournament' by PATRICK KAVANAGH, by kind permission of the Trustees of the Estate of the late Katherine B. Kavanagh, through the Jonathan Williams Literary Agency. 'The Boxers' by MICHAEL LONGLEY from *The Stairwell* (2014), by kind permission of the author and Cape Poetry, Random House, 20 Vauxhall Bridge Rd, London. 'Rope-a-Dope' by DECLAN RYAN from *Poetry* (Chicago / September 2015), by kind permission of the author and Poetry Foundation, 61 West Superior St, Chicago, IL 60654. 'The Last Glimpse of Erin' by EILÉAN NÍ CHUILLEANÁIN from *The Rose-Geranium* (1981), by kind permission of the author and The Gallery Press, Loughcrew, Oldcastle, Co Meath. 'Forty Lengths' by SINÉAD MORRISSEY from *The State of the Prisons* (2005), by kind permission of the author and Carcanet Press, Alliance House, 30 Cross St, Manchester. 'Learning to Dive' by PAT BORAN from *The Next Life* (2012), by kind permission of the author and Dedalus Press, 13 Moyclare Rd, Baldoyle, Dublin 13. 'Saturday in the Pool' by LEONTIA FLYNN from *Drives* (2008), by kind permission of the author and Cape Poetry, Random House, 20 Vauxhall Bridge Rd, London. 'The End of the Line' by CONOR O'CALLAGHAN from *The Sun King* (2013), by kind permission of the author and The Gallery Press, Loughcrew, Oldcastle, Co Meath. 'Swimming Out' by GERRY MURPHY from *End of Part One: New and Selected Poems* (2006), by kind permission of the author and Dedalus Press, 13 Moyclare Rd, Baldoyle, Dublin 13. 'Surfing' by MARY O'MALLEY from *A Perfect V* (2006), by kind permission of the author and Carcanet Press, Alliance House, 30 Cross St, Manchester. 'The One-Armed Crucifixion' by PAUL DURCAN from *Life is a Dream: 40 Years Reading Poems 1967-2007* (Harvill Secker, 2009), by kind permission of the author and Rogers, Coleridge and White, 20 Powis Mews, London, W11 1JN. 'Camogie' by MICHAEL GORMAN from *Waiting for the Sky to Fall* (1984), by kind permission of the author and Lighthouse Press, Galway. 'Camogie Match' by PATRICK KAVANAGH, by kind permission of the Trustees of the Estate of the late

ACKNOWLEDGEMENTS

Katherine B. Kavanagh, through the Jonathan Williams Literary Agency. 'Ecstasis' by JOHN FITZGERALD, by kind permission of the author. 'Donal Foley Played Hurling with my Father' by LIAM MURPHY from *Poetry Ireland Review* 3 (1981), by kind permission of the author. 'A Song for Christy Ring' by BRYAN MACMAHON, novelist, short story writer, balladeer, born Listowel, 1909–1989, by kind permission of Maurice MacMahon. 'Learning My Father's Memories' by THEO DORGAN from *Nine Bright Shiners* (2014), by kind permission of the author and Dedalus Press, 13 Moyclare Rd, Baldoyle, Dublin 13. 'Lament for Christy Ring' by BILLY RAMSELL from *The Architect's Dream of Winter* (2013), by kind permission of the author and Dedalus Press, 13 Moyclare Rd, Baldoyle, Dublin 13. 'On My Father's Birthday' by ENDA WYLEY from *Borrowed Space* (2014), by kind permission of the author and Dedalus Press, 13 Moyclare Rd, Baldoyle, Dublin 13. 'A Laminated Hurley' by TOM FRENCH from *Midnightstown* (2014), by kind permission of the author and The Gallery Press, Loughcrew, Oldcastle, Co Meath. 'American Football in Booterstown Park' by FRANK MCGUINNESS from *In a Town of Five Thousand People* (2012), by kind permission of the author and The Gallery Press, Loughcrew, Oldcastle, Co Meath. 'Game Night' by CONOR O'CALLAGHAN from *The Sun King* (2013), by kind permission of the author and The Gallery Press, Loughcrew, Oldcastle, Co Meath. 'Tagging the Stealer' by GREG DELANTY from *Collected Poems: 1986-2006* (2006), by kind permission of the author and Carcanet Press, Alliance House, 30 Cross St, Manchester. 'Chunkey' by PAUL MULDOON from the *Guardian* (10/07/2010), by kind permission of the author. 'Rugby Football Excursion' by LOUIS MACNEICE from *Collected Poems* (2007), by kind permission of the author's estate and Faber and Faber, Bloomsbury House, 74-77 Great Russell St, London. 'Team Photo' by JOHN O'DONNELL from *On Water* (2014), by kind permission of the author and Dedalus Press, 13 Moyclare Rd, Baldoyle, Dublin 13. 'The Cappoquin Cricket XI' by TOM MCCARTHY from *Mr Dineen's Careful Parade* (1999), by kind permission of the author and Anvil Press, Neptune House, 70 Royal Hill Rd, London. 'Offering the Light' by GERARD FANNING from *Hombre: New and Selected Poems* (2009), by kind permission of the author and Dedalus Press, 13 Moyclare Rd, Baldoyle, Dublin 13. 'At Master McGrath's Grave' by PAUL MULDOON from *Mules* (1977), by kind permission of the author and Faber and Faber, Bloomsbury House, 74-77 Great Russell St, London. 'Night Music' by CIARAN CARSON from *From Elsewhere* (2014), by kind permission of the author and The Gallery Press, Loughcrew, Oldcastle, Co Meath. 'The Holy Land' by MAURICE RIORDAN from *The Holy Land* (2007), by kind permission of the author and Faber and Faber, Bloomsbury House, 74-77 Great Russell St, London.